Unleash The Greatness in Your Child

Powerful,

Character–Building,

Positive

Parenting Activities

An "I Care" Positive Parenting Workbook

Written by Elbert D. Solomon, Thelma S. Solomon, and Martha Ray Dean
Book design and illustrations by Phillip L. Harper, Jr.

ISBN: 1–891187–04–X
2nd Grade; First Edition
Copyright© 2006 by "I Care" Products & Services
E–mail: parents5@icarenow.com
www.icarenow.com/parents.html
All rights reserved. Printed in the U.S.A.

Table of Contents

January

Hard Work   1

February

Humility   13

March

Accept Recognition   25

April

Value Differences   37

May

Be Cautious   51

June

Have Compassion   63

July

Be Dependable   75

August

Oversee the School Environment   87

September

Listening   99

October

Optimism   113

November

Fairness   125

December

Loyalty   137

Introduction

The "Unleash the Greatness in Your Child" Workbook

The "Unleash the Greatness in Your Child" Workbook will not only increase the impact that you can have on the social, emotional, and academic growth of your children, but it can help them to reach their fullest potential. Highly successful individuals share a number of traits in common. Among them are the thinking skills, attitudes, and behavior patterns that represent "character." This book provides tools for parents like you who want to begin unleashing the potential in their children through the development of their character.

Positive Parenting

Positive parenting strengthens parent/child relationships by engaging children with the most important teachers they will ever have—their parents. Furthermore, it increases academic achievement and expectations for the future; instills self–esteem and confidence; and reduces behavior problems and school absenteeism.

Character Development

Character development doesn't just happen, it is primarily learned from role models and significant adults and should be started at an early age. A list of the twelve "Pillars of Character" upon which the "I Care" approach is based is found on pages iv and v, along with the behaviors that define them at each grade level of the "I Care" Positive Parenting Workbooks.

"I Care"

Beginning over ten years ago, "I Care" is committed to communicating with parents the importance of their involvement with their children and helping them improve their parenting skills. Today, "I Care" is used by over a million parents.

"I Care" Positive Parenting & Mentoring Curricula

"I Care" Positive Parenting & Mentoring Curricula are used in over 35,000 classrooms for Toddler and Pre–K through High School. Activities similar to the ones in this Workbook are implemented by parents throughout the school year. Administrators, teachers, and parents have all raved about the results.

Feedback

Feedback is one of the key components to the "I Care" approach. Defining parental involvement as the number of positive interactions you have with your child makes it easy. The *Reflection Activity* at the end of each month will help you keep track of your involvement. The other indicator will be the changes you see in your child. They will be stunning.

Copyright© 2006 "I Care" Products & Services   (2nd Grade)

How To Use This Book

Practice, Practice, Practice
Practice is necessary for a behavior or attitude to become a habit. That's why we provide so many activities for each character trait. In fact, learning theory tells us that it generally takes 21 days of practice before a new habit is acquired. But don't stop with ours! Be creative in developing your own activities as well.

Discuss, Discuss, Discuss
Discuss—not tell, tell, tell—is the rule. If a child can talk about an idea using his own words, ask questions about it, and consider it from different points of view, he will both learn it and understand it more completely.

Parenting Activities
Carefully read through the month's activities. Designate a visible location to place the positive message and post the activities (refrigerator, message board, etc.). The activities can be done while walking or riding in the car, at the breakfast table, at bedtime, on weekends, and in other situations where you and your child are together. Take advantage of the "teachable moments" and read to and with your child daily.

Monthly Character Traits
There are twelve important character traits, one for each month of the year, spiraling from a Pillar of Character. They instill self–esteem, positive attitudes, and self–confidence. Focus on one character trait per month and complete the associated parenting, enrichment, reinforcement, positive message (monthly character trait), and reflection activities.

Parenting Pledge
The *Parenting Pledge* is an affirmation from the parent to the child that the character traits will be practiced and reinforced. Display it in a visible location. (See page vii.)

Child's Pledge
The *Child's Pledge* is an affirmation from the child to the parents. Have your child repeat it often until it is committed to memory. Display it in your child's room. (See page ix.)

Enrichment Activities
The *Enrichment Activities* will get your child excited and motivated about learning. The activities are designed to enhance your child's skills in reading, writing, constructing, designing, recognizing, visualizing, making patterns, and communicating.

Positive Messages
The monthly *Positive Message* should be displayed in a visible location to help your

child maintain focus on one character trait while you, as a parent, provide reinforcement actions.

Reinforcement Activities

These *Reinforcement Activities* will give parent and child multiple opportunities to manipulate and model the behaviors associated with each character trait during the month.

Reading Activities

The recommended books and reading activities support the child's literacy development and reinforce the monthly character traits. These books may be available at your local library or they can be purchased in a set of 12 at www.icarenow.com/parents.html. Other books that reinforce the month's concept may be used if the recommended books are unavailable.

Reflection Activity

The monthly *Reflection Activity* is designed for parents to summarize their positive actions, recognize their accomplishments, and encourage self–initiation of more positive parent/child interactions.

Successful Parenting Practices

The timeless successful parenting practices at the end of each month's activities were used as a guide to develop the "I Care" Positive Parenting Workbook. They serve as models for effective parent/child relationships.

12 Universal Pillars of Character

Goal Setting—*Learning How to Plan*

Self–Aware—*Understanding What You Think and Why*

Value Achievement—*Taking Pride in Accomplishments*

Value Others—*Being Able to See the Good in Everyone*

Self–Control—*Keeping Action and Emotion in Check*

Caring—*Respecting Others' Feelings and Giving of One's Self*

Responsible—*Following Through on Commitments*

Citizenship—*Showing Loyalty to the Rights of Others*

Life–Long Learner—*Enhancing Learning Skills*

Self–Confidence—*Trusting in Your Own Abilities*

Respect—*Showing Honor or Esteem*

Trustworthiness—*Being Honest*

"I Care" Positive Parenting Workbooks

- Built on twelve universally recognized pillars of good character with spiraling grade–level character traits to build one behavior on another
- Includes the primary behaviors that define each character trait for the repetition that enables transfer of learning
- Includes parenting/mentoring, enrichment, reinforcement, visual learning, and reflection activities
- Additional grade–level workbooks are available for the grades listed below

Month	Pillars of Character	Pre–K	Kinder-garten	1st Grade	2nd Grade	3rd Grade	4th Grade	5th Grade	6th Grade
January	Goal–Setting	Dream	Dream	Imagine	Hard Work	Persevere	Persist	Set Goals	Plan
February	Self–Aware	Recognize Feelings	Recognize Feelings	Sensitive	Humility	Consistency	Monitor Thinking	Integrity	Set Personal Standards
March	Value Achievement	Recognize Achievement	Recognize Achievement	Accomplishments	Accept Recognition	Dedication	Appreciation	Productive Thinking	Push Limits of Abilities
April	Value Others	Unique Qualities	Unique Qualities	Make Friends	Value Differences	Hospitable	Forgiveness	Loyalty	Tolerance
May	Self–Control	Self–Control	Self–Control	Self–Discipline	Cautious	Punctual	Endurance	Control Impulses	Respond to Feedback
June	Caring	Caring	Caring	Respect	Compassion	Gentle	Generous	Sympathetic	Dependability
July	Responsible	Responsible	Responsible	Follow Procedures	Dependable	Prudence	Thorough	Accuracy	Willing to Accept Blame
August	Citizenship	Positive Attitude Toward School	Positive Attitude Toward School	School Pride	Oversee Environment	Understand Consequences	Thriftiness	Cooperation	Stands for Right
September	Life–Long Learner	Read	Read	Discover	Listen	Alertness	Creative	Find Facts	Express Feelings
October	Self–Confidence	Self–Confidence	Self–Confidence	Self–Reliance	Optimism	Courage	Joyful	Problem Solving	Right Choices
November	Respect	Courteous	Courteous	Polite	Fairness	Patience	Honor	Open–Minded	Positive Attitude
December	Trustworthy	Honest	Honest	Sincere	Loyalty	Truthful	Reliable	Self–Knowledge	Virtuous

A Proven Educational Method

"I Care" follows best strategies of the teaching and learning process described below and has been professionally developed using relevant research.

Advanced Organizers

The *Message to Parents* is provided for introducing the month's character trait.

Three Essential Learning Conditions

These have been identified by cognitive psychologists and embedded into the workbook: reception, availability, and activation.

1. Reception—Advanced organizers focus the child's attention on specific activities.
2. Availability—Parents can take advantage of the "teachable moments" and insert parenting activities into the home schedule at any time.
3. Activation—When parents role model the character traits and ask questions such as those provided in the preplanned activities, they are activating the child's cognitive assimilation of the trait.

Repetition, Repetition, Repetition

Long–term memory is enhanced by the number of times a child mentally manipulates a trait. "I Care" provides varied repetitions of each character trait over an extended period of time. Learning theory tells us that it generally takes 21 days of practice before a new habit is acquired.

Use of Questioning Strategies

Most of the "I Care" Activities are written in the form of open–ended questions.

Connected to Real Life

Children are able to respond to activity questions (passive activity) utilizing their own experiences, and when activities involve doing something (active activity), children carry out the activity within a familiar environment that is part of their daily lives.

Substantive Conversation

Research shows that a child must talk about an idea or trait using his or her own words, ask questions about it, and look at it from multiple points of view for it to be assimilated to the point that the trait transfers into automatic behavior response. The "I Care" Workbook has built–in opportunities for all these kinds of conversations.

"I Care" Positive Parenting Pledge

I Pledge To Teach My Child:

The Importance of Hard Work

The Importance of Humility

How to Accept Recognition

How to Value Differences

How to Be Cautious

How to Have Compassion

How to Be Dependable

How to Oversee the School Environment

How to Listen

The Importance of Optimism

The Importance of Fairness

The Importance of Loyalty

Tear out this page and display the Parenting
Pledge on the other side in a visible location.

"I Care" Positive Child's Pledge

I Pledge To:

Do My Best to Achieve in School

Read Daily for Information or Enjoyment

Have a Positive Attitude Toward School

Listen to My Parent's Advice

Use Good Manners

Practice Common Courtesies

Limit My Television Watching

Be Responsible for My Actions

Stick With a Task Until It Is Finished

Tear out this page and display the Child's
Pledge on the other side in a visible location.

Parenting Activities

Message to Parents

"Dot com kids" is a new term used by psychologists to describe the children who learn how to use computers and program VCR's before they can read and write. One thing common to these children is lack of patience. Now, more than ever, parents need to teach the value of hard work and delayed gratification.

1. COMMUNICATION

The Value of Hard Work

Several things give children the impression that hard work is something to avoid. One is the message on television that work is drudgery and something to be avoided rather than accomplished. Another is how easily people seem to get what they want (credit cards are a problem here). Talk with your child about how important it is to work hard and do a job well. You'll reach your goal, learn things you need to know, save money for the future, and feel good about yourself.

2. ROLE PLAYING

Model It

Let your child see you working hard at home and on the job. Let him know that you get satisfaction out of your hard work. It makes it possible for you to provide for the family and share what you have with others.

Parenting Activities

3. TABLE TALK

Talk About It

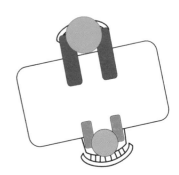

Discuss the following with your child:

- Ask your child to explain the saying "If at first you don't succeed, try, try again."
- Tell the story of *The Hare and the Tortoise* to your child and ask him what "slow and steady wins the race" means to him. What has he accomplished by working slowly and steadily?

4. WRITING

I Like to Work Hard

Help your child create a book depicting his hard work. Begin with a blank piece of 8 ½ x 11 paper and fold it in thirds across the short side. You now have six "pages," front and back. On each page, have your child draw a picture of himself doing something that is hard for him. Then, have him describe what he is doing as you act as scribe for him. Share the book with family and friends. See the example on page 5.

Hard Work

Parenting Activities

5. PHYSICAL

Sticking to It

What physical challenge do we face that requires hard work? Staying in shape or opening the pesky packaging of shrink wrapped, plastic sealed merchandise? We all face them. Help your child find a challenge and meet it through hard work. Perhaps it's riding a bike, becoming better at a favorite sport, learning to dance, or playing the piano.

6. READING

Working Hard

Read *I Want to Be a Teacher* by Dan Liebman with your child. Ask him to describe some of the many ways his teacher works hard, such as preparing lessons, giving attention to the whole class, keeping the room interesting and orderly, going to meetings, etc.

Parenting Activities

7. COMMUNITY

Going to Work

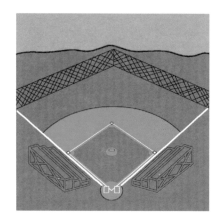

Take your child to work with you and visit friends and family members at work. Talk about how each job is different, but how all involve hard work and dedication to do well. Take pictures of your child with workers on the job. Display the pictures and talk about the jobs he likes the best.

Successful Parenting Practices

- Be sure that what you ask your child to do is appropriate for his age. Nothing frustrates a child more than being asked to do something he isn't capable of doing.

Copyright© 2006 "I Care" Products & Services   (2nd Grade)

Activity 1: Writing-Accordion Book

You can use the example below for the *Writing Activity* on page 2.

Enrichment Activity

Activity 2: Art—Lessons from History

The *Lewis and Clark Expedition* was sent out in 1803 to explore the western territories and find routes that others might later follow. They traveled thousands of miles on foot and horseback and faced the challenges of the weather, unknown terrain, hunger, sickness, and hostile tribes. Find out more about Lewis and Clark at www.nationalgeographic.com/lewisandclark/ or from your local library. Then, have your child create a picture showing how hard people from the expedition worked to survive (building shelters, hunting game, building boats, carving out canoes, taking care of their sick and wounded, etc.).

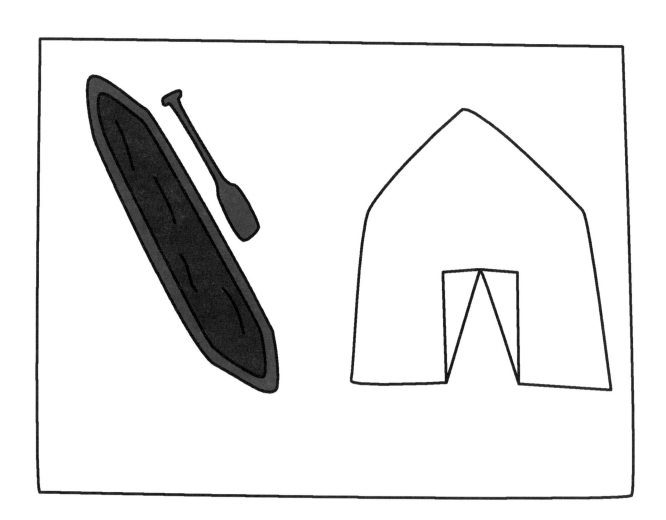

Hard Work

Enrichment Activity

Activity 3: Project—How Much Do I Have?

Most children today expect to be able to get what they want—a new toy or the latest kind of sneakers—almost as soon as it comes out. They don't understand about *earning* an allowance or *saving* for a new video game. Help your child develop an appreciation for what he has by having to work to get it. The next time he wants something new, tell him he will have to earn part of the money. Use the chart on the next page for planning how to earn money and for keeping track of progress. Mark off how much your child needs to earn on the large thermometer, then have him fill it in as he saves his money (see example below). It's guaranteed that he will be proud of himself when he's reached

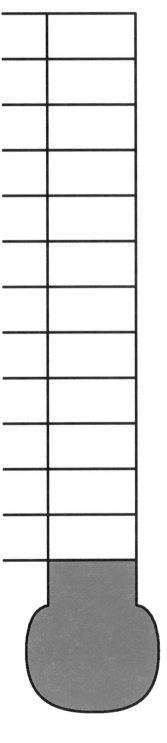

50
45
40
35
30
25
20
15
10
5

Hard Work

Saving Up Is Hard Work

What I want to buy: _____

How much does it cost?: _____

How I'm going to earn the money:

1. _____

2. _____

3. _____

4. _____

5. _____

6. _____

7. _____

8. _____

9. _____

10. _____

Hard Work

Positive Message

Activity 4: Visual Learning

Discuss with your child the connection between the two pictures below the positive message. Post the message in a visible location for your child to see it often during the month. At the end of the month, complete *Activity 5* on the other side of this sheet.

You can achieve greatness when you work hard and smart.

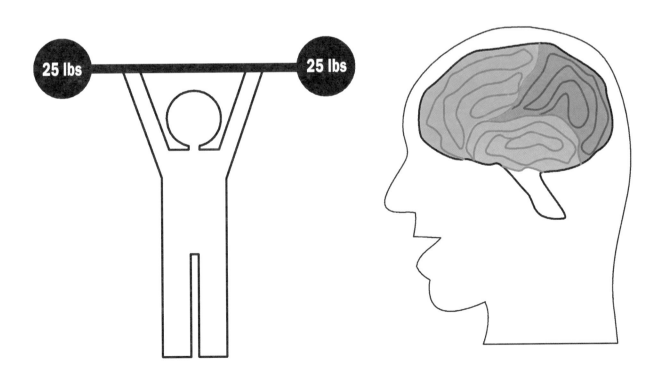

Hard Work

Reinforcement Activity

Activity 5: Things I Work Hard At . . .

Record the things your child works hard at and post in a visible location.

1. _____

2. _____

3. _____

4. _____

5. _____

Reflection Activity

Activity 6: Reflection Log

Summarize your child's positive interactions during the month and reward yourself for a job well done.

Child's Name _____ **Date** _____

Name of Parent(s) _____

Record the number for each of the following questions in the box on the right.

A. How many of the workbook activities did you do with your child?

B. How many positive recognitions did your child receive from teachers, family members, friends, etc.?

C. How many positive recognitions did your child receive from you, the parent(s)?

Hard Work

D. Record five self–initiated positive activities you did with your child that were not in this month's workbook activities.

1. _____

    _____

2. _____

    _____

3. _____

    _____

4. _____

    _____

5. _____

    _____

Parenting Activities

Message to Parents

Humility, one of the most important virtues, can't be taught directly. It is learned by example and experience. At this age, you are laying the groundwork as you teach respect, kindness, service, and honor.

1. COMMUNICATION

No Bragging

Humility doesn't mean that you deny your abilities. Humble people actually recognize their strengths and abilities. However, they realize that other people have strengths as well and don't hold themselves up as better than anyone else. Talk with your child about the importance of not bragging or putting other children down who can't perform as well as she can. If your child is teased by others, help her recognize some of her unique strengths.

2. ROLE PLAYING

Model It

An arrogant person thinks he is always right, while a humble person admits his mistakes freely. Be quick to acknowledge your mistakes, and when you're in the right, don't make fun or put someone else down.

Parenting Activities

3. TABLE TALK

Talk About It

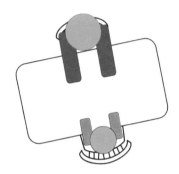

Discuss the following with your child:
- Discuss the following quote with your child: "It's the small–minded person who brags and makes fun of others. Really big people make others feel big, too."

4. WRITING

Code of Honor

Share with your child how medieval knights were not just sworn to protect their king, they had a code of honor that required that they be charitable, loyal, faithful, honest, merciful, and above all, humble. They thought it was important to be modest and submit to the greater good of humanity. They even kept their hair short as a sign of humility. Together with your child, write a "Code of Honor" for your family, following the sample on page 17.

Parenting Activities

5. PHYSICAL

It's Important to Serve

Humility is a character trait which should be valued and taught by example. Parents are advised to teach humility by searching out some unpleasant tasks, things they really don't like, and actually doing them. In other words, sacrifice what you want to do to serve others, and smile while you are doing it. Help your child to identify something that she is not fond of doing and do it along with her, such as doing someone else's chores, giving up her favorite television shows for a week so that other family members can watch theirs, or helping mom or dad with a special project instead of playing with friends.

6. READING

Expressing Feelings

After reading *Shy Charles* by Rosemary Wells with your child, have her describe the feelings that Charles expressed with his face. Have her make some of the same expressions and you guess what they represent. Then, ask her what she thinks it's like to be shy.

Parenting Activities

7. COMMUNITY

Helping Other People

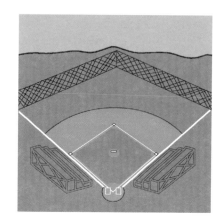

In every community there are people who serve others without seeking attention for themselves. It may be members of a service group like *Big Brothers* and *Big Sisters* or a grandmother who bakes cookies to distribute at the homeless shelter. Watch the local newspaper for stories about these good citizens and point them out to your child. You can also find out about community servants from the local library or your house of worship.

Successful Parenting Practices

- If your child receives constant praise without discipline, or is always getting what she wants when she wants it, she can become self–centered and prideful, which is the opposite of humility. Be sure to balance your praise with the expectation of good behavior and follow through.

Copyright© 2006 "I Care" Products & Services   (2nd Grade)

Humility

Enrichment Activity

Activity 1: Writing–Family Code of Honor

You can use this example for the *Writing Activity* on page 14.

Our Family Code of Honor

We pledge to do our best at all times to:

- Treat all people with respect
- Tell the truth
- Share what we have
- Show patience and kindness to others
- Follow rules and laws
- Take care of the earth by recycling, not littering, etc.
- Accept responsibility for our actions
- Do all things with humility

John Smith

Joan Smith

David Smith

Cathy Smith

Signed this day *February 2*

Enrichment Activity

Activity 2: Art—My Own Shield

The shields carried by medieval knights were a kind of code. Each color and figure had a special meaning. There were "rules" about who could use certain symbols and where symbols could be placed on the shield. The knight would design his shield to proclaim who he was and what he cared about. Using some of the information on the next page, help your child design her own coat of arms. For more information, visit the following website: www.cdli.ca/CITE/medieval_heraldry_intro.html.

Copyright© 2006 "I Care" Products & Services   (2nd Grade)

Humility

Meanings of Colors

Gold................................. Generosity and elevation of the mind
Silver or White................ Peace and sincerity
Red................................. Warrior
Blue................................ Truth and loyalty
Green .... Hope, joy
Black............................... Constancy or grief
Purple .... Royal majesty, sovereignty, and justice
Orange............................ Worthy ambition
Maroon .... Patient in battle, and yet victorious

Meanings of Symbols

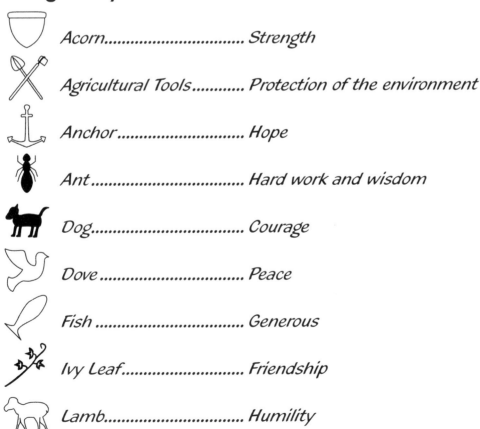

Acorn............................... Strength

Agricultural Tools............ Protection of the environment

Anchor............................. Hope

Ant.................................. Hard work and wisdom

Dog.................................. Courage

Dove .... Peace

Fish .... Generous

Ivy Leaf............................ Friendship

Lamb................................ Humility

February

Humility

Enrichment Activity

Activity 3: Project–A Family Reminder

Many people consider humility as the foundation of good character—it's the behavior you build on. Help your child design and make a "Humility Place Mat" for each member of the family. It can contain sayings about humility or pictures of children serving and showing respect to others. See the sample below to get started.

Humility makes the world a better place to live.

20

Humility

Positive Message

Activity 4: Visual Learning

Ask your child to circle the words or phrases that best define humility below the positive message. Post the message in a visible location for your child to see it often during the month. At the end of the month, complete *Activity 5* on the other side of this sheet.

You make me happy and proud when you respect the rights and feelings of others.

Caring

Respects others' feelings

Selfish

Rude

Kind

Rough

Understanding

Boastful

Says "Thank you" and "Please"

Copyright© 2006 "I Care" Products & Services   (2nd Grade)

Do Not Photocopy.

Humility

Reinforcement Activity

Activity 5: Times I Have Been Humble . . .

Record some times/situations when your child has demonstrated humility.

1. _____

2. _____

3. _____

4. _____

5. _____

Activity 6: Reflection Log

Summarize your child's positive interactions during the month and reward yourself for a job well done.

Child's Name _____ **Date** _____

Name of Parent(s) _____

Record the number for each of the following questions in the box on the right.

A. How many of the workbook activities did you do with your child? ☐

B. How many positive recognitions did your child receive from teachers, family members, friends, etc.? ☐

C. How many positive recognitions did your child receive from you, the parent(s)? ☐

February

Humility

D. Record five self–initiated positive activities you did with your child that were not in this month's workbook activities.

1. _____

   _____

2. _____

   _____

3. _____

   _____

4. _____

   _____

5. _____

   _____

Do Not Photocopy.

Copyright© 2006 "I Care" Products & Services   (2nd Grade)

Accept Recognition

Message to Parents

We don't want children to expect or need recognition all the time. When that happens, they will not learn to be self-motivated. However, we do want them to feel comfortable receiving recognition. This is especially true for children who are naturally shy. Practice will help them overcome embarrassment.

1. COMMUNICATION

Say "Thank You"

Make sure your child knows how important recognition is, even a simple "thank you." Have him imagine how he would feel if he spent hours painting a model airplane to give to a friend for his birthday and the friend just looked at the present and picked up another one to open. We don't do something kind in order to get recognition, but we like to know that what we did makes someone else happy.

2. ROLE PLAYING

Model It

Be a role model daily. Recognize the accomplishments of friends and family with comments, notes, and e-mails. Ask people about what they have done and how their actions have benefited others. Share the things that you do well.

Accept Recognition

Parenting Activities

3. TABLE TALK

Talk About It

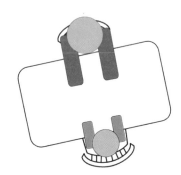

Discuss the following with your child:

- Model self–recognition. Say out loud things you do well. Examples could be "I fry the best chicken in town!"; "I'm a terrific parent."; "I keep the car sparkling clean!"; etc.
- Ask your child how his teacher recognizes students in class. Who receives lots of recognition and why does he think that person is selected so much?

4. WRITING

Acceptance Speech

Help your child write an acceptance speech for the award he is going to receive (see page 30). Look at the sample on page 29 and review the parts of an acceptance speech with him. Act as scribe if he isn't able to put all he wants to say into writing.

Accept Recognition

5. PHYSICAL

"Wall of Fame"

The fear of public speaking is the number two fear of people throughout the United States (after the fear of death). One reason for this is lack of practice. Your family's "Wall of Fame" presentation provides your child with an opportunity to make a speech in front of people he knows. Help him practice his acceptance speech at least five times, more if he needs it. If you have a karaoke machine or other microphone, let him use that.

6. READING

Beautiful Results

Children's Stories

Jack's Garden by Henry Cole illustrates how one simple act, such as planting seeds, can bring beautiful results. As you go page by page with your child, enjoy the process of transformation. Mention that, as important as planting the seed was, it wasn't until it bloomed into a garden that he received recognition.

Accept Recognition

Parenting Activities

7. COMMUNITY

Awards Ceremony

Every community has awards ceremonies: the *Boy Scouts* have them, high school sports teams have them, and service clubs have them. Call the local newspaper to find out which ones are scheduled close to you and, if they are open to the public, take your child. You don't have to stay the entire time, just long enough for him to see what an awards ceremony is like.

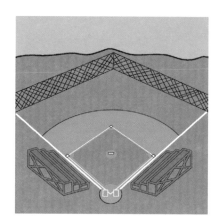

Successful Parenting Practices

- Display your child's work so that people can appreciate it. You may even want to frame some of it. When you take something down, keep it in a photo album or art portfolio. You can get cardboard portfolios at an office supply store.

Copyright© 2006 "I Care" Products & Services   (2nd Grade)

Activity 1: Writing—Acceptance Speech

Use the example below for the *Writing Activity* on page 26.

Thank you for this award.

Thank you, Mr. Simmons, for nominating me to be Volunteer of the Year.

I like to work at the Humane Society because I love animals. I like the people here, too. They have taught me a lot about taking care of dogs. I used to think that you treated old dogs and new dogs the same, but now I know that old dogs need extra things. I hope I keep learning.

Accept Recognition

Enrichment Activity

Activity 2: Project-Wall of Fame

Create a "Wall of Fame." Explain to your child that it's like the *Baseball Hall of Fame* (www.baseballhalloffame.org), where baseball players are honored for their achievements. Your family "Wall of Fame" will be used to recognize the accomplishments of all family members. Have an actual awards ceremony where each member of the family walks up, receives an award, and gives an acceptance speech. Then, hang their awards on the "Wall of Fame."

Activity 3: Art–Awards, Awards, Awards

Create a certificate for each member of the family to present at the "Awards Ceremony" for the *Community Activity* on page 28 and place them on the "Wall of Fame" (*Project Activity* on page 30). You can use the template on the next page to help you get started.

YOU DID IT!

You are the best mom in the whole world. I love you!

YOU DID IT!

Activity 4: Visual Learning

Discuss with your child how the welcome mat below the positive message can impact feelings. Post the message in a visible location for your child to see it often during the month. At the end of the month, complete *Activity 5* on the other side of this sheet.

When someone says "thank you," it's easy to smile and say "You're welcome."

Copyright© 2006 "I Care" Products & Services   (2nd Grade)

Accept Recognition

Reinforcement Activity

Activity 5: Times I Accepted Recognition . . .

Record times your child accepted recognition and post in a visible location.

1. _____

2. _____

3. _____

4. _____

5. _____

Copyright© 2006 "I Care" Products & Services (2nd Grade)

Accept Recognition

Reflection Activity

Activity 6: Reflection Log

Summarize your child's positive interactions during the month and reward yourself for a job well done.

Child's Name _____ **Date** _____

Name of Parent(s) _____

Record the number for each of the following questions in the box on the right.

A. How many of the workbook activities did you do with your child?

B. How many positive recognitions did your child receive from teachers, family members, friends, etc.?

C. How many positive recognitions did your child receive from you, the parent(s)?

Accept Recognition

D. Record five self–initiated positive activities you did with your child that were not in this month's workbook activities.

1. _____

   _____

2. _____

   _____

3. _____

   _____

4. _____

   _____

5. _____

   _____

Copyright© 2006 "I Care" Products & Services   (2nd Grade)

Value Differences

Parenting Activities

Message to Parents

With the expansion of technology throughout the world, it's quite possible our children may someday work with and for companies on the other side of the globe. The more they understand and appreciate cultural differences, the better equipped they will be for the future.

1. COMMUNICATION

The Value of Friendship

Talk to your child about the value of friendships. Describe some of the friends you have had whose ethnic background was different from yours. Share what you learned from them.

2. ROLE PLAYING

Model It

The children of today are usually multi–ethnic. For instance, Joshua's mom is Maria, an Evangelical Christian from Ecuador. His dad's name is Mohammed, a Muslim from Pakistan. They live in Queens, New York. Paulie is of Japanese heritage, but was born in Jamaica. His family later moved to Montreal and now lives in Miami. Talk with your child often about the different cultures represented in your family.

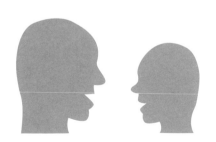

April

Value Differences

Parenting Activities

3. TABLE TALK

Talk About It

Discuss the following with your child:
* Referring to the list of holidays on page 41, discuss the different holidays that occur in the month of April. Select several to learn more about. You can do an internet search or call the librarian at your local library and ask for help.

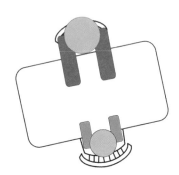

4. WRITING

What Would You Say?

People from other countries often get the wrong idea about what Americans are like because all they know is from Hollywood movies. Ask your child to pretend she is writing to a girl in China who is just her age, explaining one of the following topics. Act as scribe if she isn't able to put in writing all she has to say. Examples: (1) We don't all live in big cities. (2) The kinds of pets we have. (3) The kinds of homes we live in. (4) What we learn in school. (5) The kinds of things we do after school.

38

Do Not Photocopy.

Copyright© 2006 "I Care" Products & Services   (2nd Grade)

Value Differences

Parenting Activities

5. PHYSICAL

Outside/Inside

This simple object lesson helps children understand that we're all the same "under the skin." Start with two apples, one red and one green. Ask your child to describe each. Now cut them open (in the same direction). Talk about how they may look different on the outside but they are also the same on the inside, just like people. Everyone looks different on the outside, but it is what is inside that really counts.

6. READING

Being Different

Children's Stories

Wings, by Christopher Myers, is the story of Ikarus Jackson and how he finds acceptance despite being different. After reading it with your child, discuss some of the experiences Ikarus faced and how he coped with them.

Value Differences

Parenting Activities

7. COMMUNITY

Many Cultures

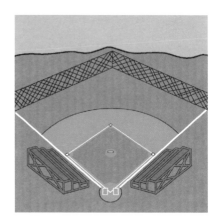

Visit the local library with your child and ask the librarian for information about the different ethnic groups in your community. Find out about the contributions each has made to the community.

Successful Parenting Practices

- When children are learning to value differences, they sometimes need to ask questions or clear up some misunderstandings. Give them room to talk. Just knowing that you are listening can be enough.

Value Differences

Enrichment Activity

Activity 1: Table Talk–Holiday Chart

Use the chart below for the *Table Talk Activity* on page 38.

April 1

Farvardin or *Sizden Bedar* (Iran)—It is the 13th day after Nowruz. The number 13 is considered an unlucky number for the Persians so everyone leaves home for the day to go on picnics or trips.

April Fool's Day (International)—This is the day everyone plays jokes on each other. It began in France and is now celebrated all over the world.

April 5

Qing Ming Festival (China, Taiwan)—On this national holiday, family graves are visited to ask for the blessings of the departed spirits.

April 8

Buddha's Birthday (International)—On this day, Buddhists celebrate in various ways depending on ethnicity and region.

April 10

Arbor Day (USA)—Communities across the United States plant trees in an ongoing effort to save American forests.

April 11

Prophet's Birthday (Islamic)—This holiday celebrates the birthday of the prophet Muhammad.

April 14–16

Sechselauten (Switzerland)—The word *Sechse-lauten* means "six o'clock chimes." When church bells ring six times, an image representing winter is burned and spring is welcomed.

April 21

Gathering of Nations Pow Wow (Albuquerque, NM, USA)—More than 600 Native American tribes and nations participate in a three–day celebration.

April 22

Earth Day (International)—Begun in 1970, this day commemorates a worldwide effort to protect the planet, children, and the future of mankind.

April 23

Children's Day (Turkey)—Throughout the country, students are elected by their classmates to study and take over the government for a day. Children are treated to free ice cream, free movies, and free transportation for the day.

April 25

Yom HaShoah (Jewish)—It is held every year in remembrance of the approximately six million Jews who died in the Holocaust.

April 27

Freedom Day (South Africa)—On this day, the first all–race election took place and South Africans brought Nelson Mandela into political power in 1994.

April 29

Midori no hi (Japan)—This holiday is also known as *Greenery Day* to appreciate nature.

Passover, Good Friday, and Easter are also usually celebrated in April.

Value Differences

Enrichment Activity

Activity 2: Art–The Many Faces of Friendship

Provide the materials your child will need to create a mobile full of friends. She will need the faces on the next page, crayons or markers, seven 5" pieces of yarn or string (enough for each face, plus three), three bamboo skewers with pointed ends cut off (about a foot long each). You may want to cut a notch about 1" from each end of the skewer to prevent the strings from slipping.

1. Using the templates on the next page, have your child draw on and color the face of each of her friends. Punch out the hole in the top of the faces and attach a string to each.

2. Tie two of the faces to each end of one of the skewers. Then, tie a string to the middle of the skewer.

3. Tie the other end of the middle string to the end of another skewer. Then, tie another face to the end of the skewer. Next, tie a string to the middle of the skewer.

4. Tie the middle string to the end of the remaining skewer. Then, tie the remaining face to the other end of the skewer. Finally, tie a string to the middle of the last skewer and hang the mobile in your child's room or somewhere the family can enjoy it.

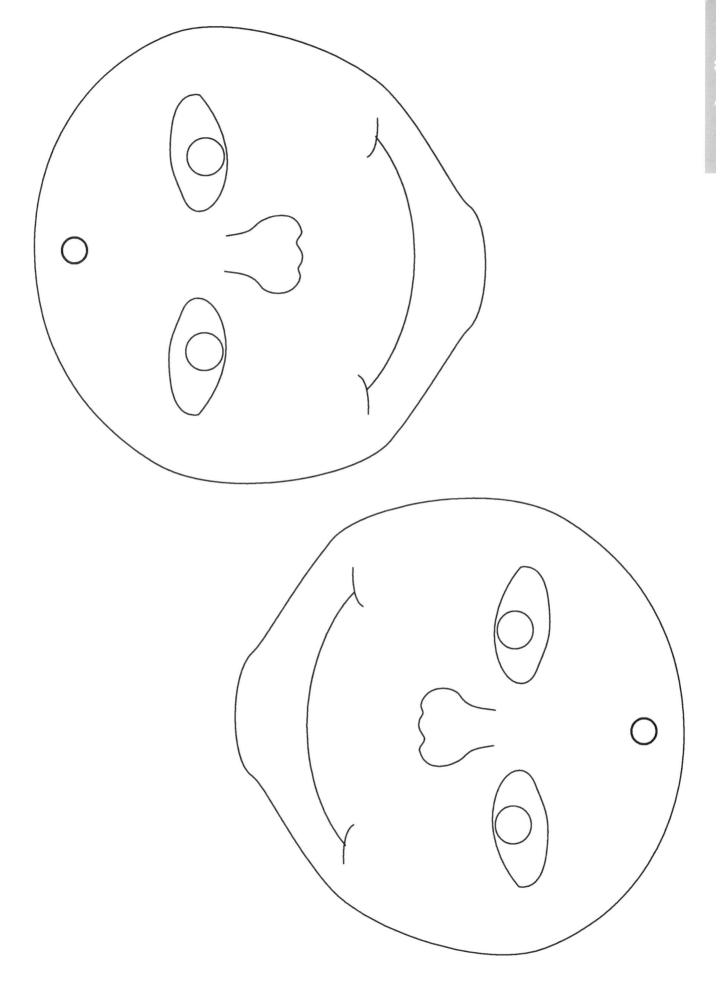

Cut out the faces on the other side of this page for the Art Activity.

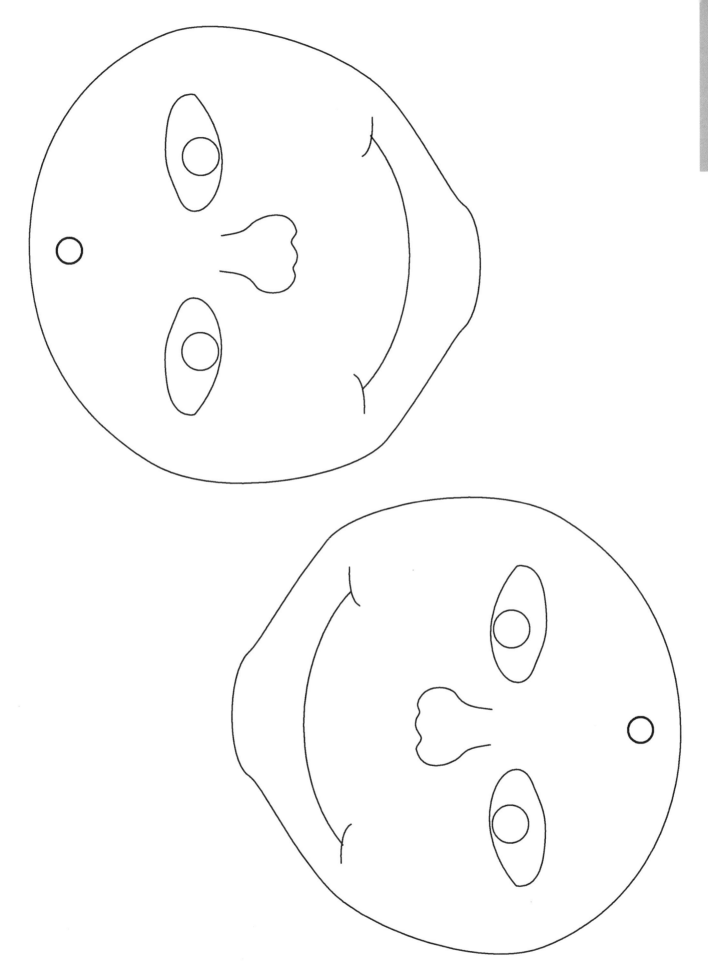

45

Value Differences

Cut out the faces on the other side of this page for the Art Activity.

Value Differences

Activity 3: Visual Learning

Ask your child to share what she has learned from her friends and record it in the circles below the positive message. Post the message in a visible location for your child to see it often during the month. At the end of the month, complete *Activity 4* on the other side of this sheet.

Friends may be different colors and sizes. We can all learn from each other.

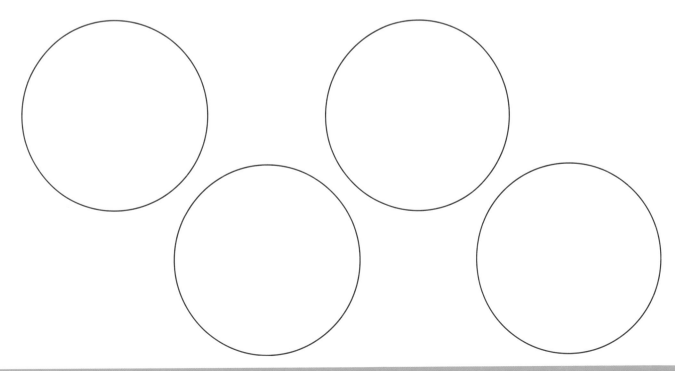

Value Differences

Reinforcement Activity

Activity 4: What I Like About My Friends

Record what your child likes about her friends and post in a visible location.

1. _____

2. _____

3. _____

4. _____

5. _____

Value Differences

Activity 5: Reflection Log

Summarize your child's positive interactions during the month and reward yourself for a job well done.

Child's Name _____ **Date** _____

Name of Parent(s) _____

Record the number for each of the following questions in the box on the right.

A. How many of the workbook activities did you do with your child?

B. How many positive recognitions did your child receive from teachers, family members, friends, etc.?

C. How many positive recognitions did your child receive from you, the parent(s)?

Copyright© 2006 "I Care" Products & Services   (2nd Grade)

Value Differences

D. Record five self–initiated positive activities you did with your child that were not in this month's workbook activities.

1. _____

    _____

2. _____

    _____

3. _____

    _____

4. _____

    _____

5. _____

    _____

Copyright© 2006 "I Care" Products & Services   (2nd Grade)

Message to Parents

Caution is taking care to avoid danger or harm. It isn't just learning rules of what to do and not to do. It is being observant and thinking smart. These are things you can teach your child.

1. COMMUNICATION

Be Cautious

Discuss the meaning of the word *caution* and talk with your child about the need for caution. Think of examples of how you use caution at home and away from home. Emphasize that he cannot control others but can control how he reacts.

2. ROLE PLAYING

Model It

Show caution in all you do. Drive safely, make sure there are no dangers around your house, such as frayed wires or broken glass, handle tools with care, and keep all firearms under lock and key. While you are practicing safety, keep a positive attitude with your child so he will not become apprehensive or constantly concerned about danger. Fear can cause him to freeze when he needs to be cautious.

Be Cautious

Parenting Activities

3. TABLE TALK

Talk About It

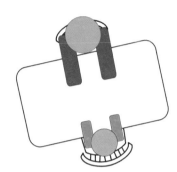

Discuss the following with your child:
- Talk with your child about what he should do if he gets home and finds the door ajar or a window broken, someone has eaten something poisonous, the doorbell rings and mom is in the shower, or a stranger asks for his name and address.
- Practice the actions your child might take for the situations above. Add other scenarios your child might face.

4. WRITING

Funny Feelings

Safety experts say that instinct is one of the best protections against danger. Talk with your child about the funny feelings you get when something doesn't feel safe. Think of the things that might cause this feeling: someone being too friendly, being touched or hugged the wrong way, when someone slows down or stops near you in a vehicle, strangers who ask for help. Act as scribe while your child describes some of the funny feelings he's gotten in the past.

Copyright© 2006 "I Care" Products & Services   (2nd Grade)

Be Cautious

Parenting Activities

5. PHYSICAL

Scream!

Children need to know that there are times it's okay to scream at the top of their lungs. Go back over the list of funny feelings that your child made in the writing activity. Would screaming be an appropriate response for any of them? Practice how to scream. "No. Get away!" or "This is not my mother!" To avoid causing fear in your child with an activity like this, talk about how he has to know some rules if he wants to earn more freedom, to walk in the mall with friends or down to a neighbor's house.

6. READING

Find the Magic

After reading *The Magic Fan* by Keith Baker with your child, discuss Yoshi's great discovery. Where did he find the magic?

Be Cautious

Parenting Activities

7. COMMUNITY

It Takes Work

Take your child to a sports event. While you are watching, talk about the kind of self–discipline athletes must have in order to develop their skills, even when they have natural talent. Discuss how important it is for them to be cautious to prevent injuries.

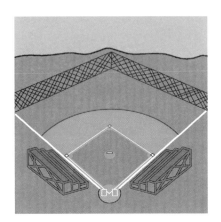

Successful Parenting Practices

- With all the media attention given to violence against children, you may want to assure your child that what's in the news is not what happens all the time. Fearful children are easier to spot and victimize.

Copyright© 2006 "I Care" Products & Services   (2nd Grade)

Be Cautious

Activity 1: Art—In Case of Emergency

Have your child create an "In Case of Emergency" poster that all the family can use. Post the following information:

- Home address and phone number
- Directions to your house
- Parents' work and cell numbers
- Emergency (911)
- Poison Control Center (1–800–222–1222)
- Grandparents and neighbors along with telephone numbers
- Your child's doctor and number
- Life threatening allergies that anyone may have
- Medications that emergency workers would need to know about

Label the telephone numbers with identifying pictures so that someone in a panic will be more likely to dial the correct number. Make sure there is a copy of the poster at each phone.

In Case of Emergency

Home: 273 N. West St.

Phone: 222-5555

Emergency: 911

Poison Control: 1-800-222-1222

Grandma: 223-1234

Dr. Smith: 222-4444

Chris is allergic to peanuts.

Dad takes insulin.

55

Be Cautious

Enrichment Activity

Activity 2: Project—Become an Observer

Help your child become an expert observer. Begin with putting a collection of 10–12 familiar items on a table and covering them so he can't see what's there. Tell him he will have 10 seconds to memorize as many of the objects as he can. Remove the cover for 10 seconds. Once the objects are covered again, ask him to list the objects. Do this periodically, increasing the number of objects and using less familiar items. Now, take this observation game into the community. Cut out the game cards on this page, stick them in your car, and play from time to time.

Observation Challenge #1 (In the Car)
- *Where is the street sign?*
- *What is the name of the street we're on?*
- *Count the traffic lights until I say stop.*
- *Look at the license number of the car in front of us. See how much of it you can remember in 10 seconds. (Silently count to 10, then tell your child to close his eyes and tell the number back to you.)*

Observation Challenge #2 (What Color Was It?)
Ask your child to watch out the window as you drive. Without taking your eyes off the road, direct his attention to vehicles you pass.
- *What color was that van we just passed?*
- *How many people were in the van?*
- *How many doors are on that truck?*
- *What color was the sign on that truck?*

Observation Challenge #3 (Give Me the Details)
Do this challenge at the mall. After you've come out of a store, ask you child:
- *Tell me everything you can remember about the person who waited on us.*
- *What did I say to the clerk?*
- *How many people were in line at the check out? Describe them.*

Observation Challenge #4 (What Did They Look Like?)
You can do this anywhere you will be seeing strangers.
- *See the man over there? Tell me what he looks like.*
- *What was the clerk wearing?*
- *How many people just passed us?*
- *What color was the woman's hair who just passed us?*

Activity 3: Project—Sign Identification

Make sure your child is familiar with the signs below. Ask him to cut them out and place them in the needed locations at home. He can personalize the signs with his own statements of caution.

57

Be Cautious

Cut out the signs on the other side of this page for the Project Activity.

Be Cautious

Positive Message

Activity 4: Visual Learning

Discuss with your child what each of the symbols below the positive message means. Post the message in a visible location for your child to see it often during the month. At the end of the month, complete *Activity 5* on the other side of this sheet.

Caution is avoiding danger. I'm proud that you are cautious.

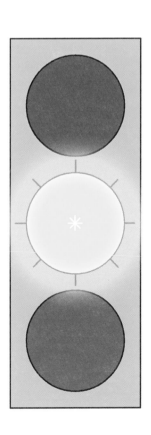

Be Cautious

Reinforcement Activity

Activity 5: I Am Cautious When I . . .

Record examples of when your child has been cautious and post in a visible location.

1. _____

2. _____

3. _____

4. _____

5. _____

Copyright© 2006 "I Care" Products & Services   (2nd Grade)

Be Cautious

Activity 6: Reflection Log

Summarize your child's positive interactions during the month and reward yourself for a job well done.

Child's Name _____ **Date** _____

Name of Parent(s) _____

Record the number for each of the following questions in the box on the right.

A. How many of the workbook activities did you do with your child?

B. How many positive recognitions did your child receive from teachers, family members, friends, etc.?

C. How many positive recognitions did your child receive from you, the parent(s)?

Be Cautious

D. Record five self–initiated positive activities you did with your child that were not in this month's workbook activities.

1. _____

   _____

2. _____

   _____

3. _____

   _____

4. _____

   _____

5. _____

   _____

Have Compassion

Parenting Activities

Message to Parents

Compassion—the ability to reach out to those who may have less than yourself—is another one of those character traits best learned by the example of parents.

1. COMMUNICATION

Make a Difference

Talk with your child about ways to make a positive difference in people's lives. Share examples of things you've done for other people and how those people benefitted.

2. ROLE PLAYING

Model It

Show compassion by visiting and calling family and friends who live alone, are elderly, sick, or in need of companionship. Talk openly about how small acts of kindness can make a big difference in someone's life.

Have Compassion

Parenting Activities

3. TABLE TALK

Talk About It

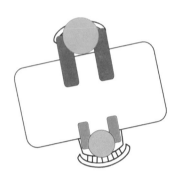

Discuss the following with your child:
- Practice with your child some of the things she can say in the following situations: (1) a friend's pet just died; (2) a schoolmate is being teased all of the time; (3) your next door neighbor is an older lady who has no family in town.
- If you could pick one person to help, who would it be and what would you do?

4. WRITING

Learning to Love

The animated movie *Lilo and Stitch* is about the compassion of a young girl who is living in difficult circumstances. After watching it with your child, talk about how Lilo was able to keep a positive attitude and help Stitch learn to love. Then, act as scribe while she tells you what she learned about compassion from the movie. Use page 67 for writing her responses, then hang it up.

Parenting Activities

5. PHYSICAL

Rice and Beans

Most of the people in the world survive on a diet of rice of beans. Help your child gain a greater understanding of what this is like, and how much we have compared to the rest of the world. Select a day when the family will be eating at home and serve nothing but rice and beans all day. No butter, salt, or pepper because poor people don't have them.

6. READING

Compassionate Friends

Do you remember reading *Charlotte's Web* by E. B. White? There's still nothing like it to communicate caring and compassion. Enjoy the friendship of Charlotte and Wilbur with your child and share Wilbur's fear and Charlotte's fate. Talk with your child about the scenes that were most humorous, most happy, and most sad.

Children's Stories

Parenting Activities

7. COMMUNITY

Community Compassion Project

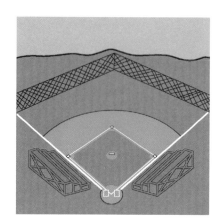

Plan and carry out a "Community Compassion" project with your child. Find out if the local hospital has a "wish list" of toys for children or call the local animal shelter to see how you can help, perhaps by raising money. In one city, children collected old cell phones to raise money. Let your child help make the choice, don't force the project on him.

Successful Parenting Practices

- Use every chance you get to help your child develop sensitivity to the experiences of others. How do the victims of a natural disaster feel? What is it like to be an overweight girl or a short, skinny boy? Sensitivity is an important component to compassion.

Activity 1: Writing—Learning to Love

Use the space below for the *Writing Activity* on page 64.

Have Compassion

Tear out this page and display what your child wrote for the Writing Activity.

Enrichment Activity

Activity 2: Project-Helping Others

Mother Teresa fed the poor and sick of Calcutta, India. She sheltered them and nursed them. But most important was the fact that she loved them. She wanted to make them feel like they were special even though they were poor. The book *Mother Teresa: Sister to the Poor* by Patricia Reilly Giff tells about all her compassion. There are also many young humanitarians who show compassion to those in need. Go over the list below, read about Mother Teresa, or talk with your child about some of the compassionate people you know. Then, act as scribe while she describes how she would like to help people in need. Record her ideas on the next page, tear out the page, and hang it where you can talk about it from time to time.

Young Humanitarians

- *One nine-year-old girl was planning her birthday. She decided she didn't need anything herself and, instead of bringing presents, she asked her friends to donate money for tsunami relief. She raised $280.*

- *A 13-year-old from the mid-west has put together over 100 health kits for the poor.*

- *Children at an after-school program in New York City's Chinatown collected over $3,100 for South Asia relief.*

- *A first grader in Tennessee organized a tsunami benefit to raise $5000.*

- *For more examples, go to www.amazing-kids.org.*

Helping Others

Activity 3: Visual Learning

In the "Free Space" below the positive message, list some caring acts you and your child can do together. Post the message in a visible location for your child to see it often during the month. At the end of the month, complete *Activity 4* on the other side of this sheet.

I get so much joy knowing that you care.

Free Space

_____

_____

_____

_____

_____

Have Compassion

Reinforcement Activity

Activity 4: Connecting With Others . . .

Record examples of times your child showed compassion for others and post in a visible location.

1. _____

2. _____

3. _____

4. _____

5. _____

Copyright© 2006 "I Care" Products & Services   (2nd Grade)

Have Compassion

Reflection Activity

Activity 5: Reflection Log

Summarize your child's positive interactions during the month and reward yourself for a job well done.

Child's Name _____ **Date** _____

Name of Parent(s) _____

Record the number for each of the following questions in the box on the right.

A. How many of the workbook activities did you do with your child?

B. How many positive recognitions did your child receive from teachers, family members, friends, etc.?

C. How many positive recognitions did your child receive from you, the parent(s)?

Copyright© 2006 "I Care" Products & Services   (2nd Grade)

Do Not Photocopy.

Have Compassion

D. Record five self–initiated positive activities you did with your child that were not in this month's workbook activities.

1. _____

   _____

2. _____

   _____

3. _____

   _____

4. _____

   _____

5. _____

   _____

Copyright© 2006 "I Care" Products & Services   (2nd Grade)

Parenting Activities

Message to Parents

Your child needs to know that doing well at work and having happy relationships required dependability: being true to your word and being responsible.

1. COMMUNICATION

What Is Dependable?

Talk with your child about what it means to be dependable (you do what you say you will without having to be reminded). Ask him how he would feel if you had promised to pick him up at school and were an hour late? What if his best friend borrowed a toy and didn't give it back when he said he would. Or imagine that he'd forgotten to close the back door tightly and your new puppy got out and got lost. Being dependable doesn't just protect out feelings, it sometimes protects our safety.

2. ROLE PLAYING

Model It

How familiar is the following scenario? You've asked your child to do his chores before going to play. Over and over, he begs out of it because his friends are waiting. "Please, please, please!" he says. And you reply "Just this once." thinking to yourself "His friends are important, I don't want to jeopardize their relationship." Now "just this once" become every time. What is the message you are sending? Your child doesn't need to be dependable and follow through on his responsibilities. Is that what you want to model for him?

Parenting Activities

3. TABLE TALK

Talk About It

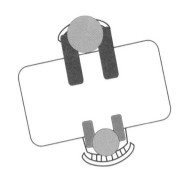

Discuss the following with your child:

- Are the children in the following situations being dependable? If not, what should they do instead? (1) Kelly was supposed to be doing her homework, but was drawing pictures. (2) Chris made sure his toys were put away every night before bed. (3) Juan was responsible for setting the table for dinner every night, but he was usually late coming home from his friend's house.

4. WRITING

Reminder Checklist

This book belongs to:

Some of us need reminders while we are developing the habits of dependability. Let your child design a reminder checklist similar to the one on page 79. Make 30 copies and use one every evening to write out the things that need to be done the next day.

Be Dependable

Parenting Activities

5. PHYSICAL

I'm Depending on You

Try this simple trust walk with the whole family. The object is for you to take turns leading each other from one end of the house to another. One of you leads while the second person is blindfolded (no peeking!). Tell your child you are depending on him to keep you from bumping into things as he guides you or gives you verbal directions.

6. READING

Right the First Time

Amelia Bedelia by Peggy Parish is a children's classic. As you read this with your child, ask in what ways Amelia was dependable (she did get all the work done!). What could have helped her get the work done right the first time?

Children's Stories

July

Be Dependable

Parenting Activities

7. COMMUNITY

What If . . .

Brainstorm with your child a list of community workers and talk about what would happen if they were not dependable. Examples could be policemen (some criminals might get away), firemen (buildings might burn down), sanitation workers, paramedics, etc.

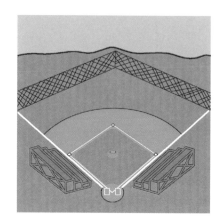

Successful Parenting Practices

- While your child is still learning about dependability, give him a second chance if he forgets to do something he was supposed to do. But don't let him out of doing it. You could say "Remember that being dependable means doing something without being reminded. I'm going to remind you this time, but next time, it's up to you." Then follow through with what you say.

Be Dependable

Enrichment Activity

Activity 1: Writing-Reminder Checklist

Use the checklist below for the *Writing Activity* on page 76.

I'll Do It! You Can Depend on It!

Get Ready for School

_____ Homework

_____ Lunch

_____ Notes

_____ Money

Chores to Do _____

_____

Before School _____

_____

After School _____

_____

Other _____

_____

Be Dependable

Enrichment Activities

Activity 2: Project—Taking Care of a Pet

Pets depend on us to take care of them. Talk with your child about what a pet owner would need to do if he had a dog, cat, bird, etc. Write down what your child needs to do daily, monthly, and yearly to take care of his pet. If you do not have a family pet, make a list of things your child can do to care for the wild birds in your yard or in the neighborhood park, then help him do them.

Activity 3: Art—Cartoon

Have your child draw a picture of your family on the "Trust Walk" from the *Physical Activity* on page 77. He can use the boxes on the next page to make a cartoon of the "Trust Walk." In each frame, he can tell more of the story. Hang the picture for all to enjoy!

Copyright© 2006 "I Care" Products & Services   (2nd Grade)

Here's What Happened on the "Trust Walk"

1.

2.

3.

4.

Be Dependable

Tear out this page and display the cartoons your child drew for the Art Activity

Be Dependable

Activity 4: Visual Learning

Discuss with your child ways to become more dependable as he grows up. Post the message in a visible location for your child to see it often during the month. At the end of the month, complete *Activity 5* on the other side of this sheet.

You're growing up. I'm proud that I can depend on you.

Copyright© 2006 "I Care" Products & Services   (2nd Grade)

Do Not Photocopy.

Be Dependable

Reinforcement Activity

Activity 5: I Am Dependable When . . .

Record examples of when your child demonstrated he was dependable and post in a visible location.

1. _____

2. _____

3. _____

4. _____

5. _____

Copyright© 2006 "I Care" Products & Services   (2nd Grade)

Be Dependable

Reflection Activity

Activity 6: Reflection Log

Summarize your child's positive interactions during the month and reward yourself for a job well done.

Child's Name _____ **Date** _____

Name of Parent(s) _____

Record the number for each of the following questions in the box on the right.

A. How many of the workbook activities did you do with your child?

B. How many positive recognitions did your child receive from teachers, family members, friends, etc.?

C. How many positive recognitions did your child receive from you, the parent(s)?

Be Dependable

D. Record five self–initiated positive activities you did with your child that were not in this month's workbook activities.

1. _____

_____

2. _____

_____

3. _____

_____

4. _____

_____

5. _____

_____

Copyright© 2006 "I Care" Products & Services   (2nd Grade)

Oversee the School Environment

Parenting Activities

Message to Parents

Everyone has a responsibility to care for the school environment. With early training, it can become a lifestyle.

---

1. COMMUNICATION

I'm Just One Person

Some people assume that because they are just one person, it won't matter if they litter and, besides, it's not their responsibility. Help your child to recognize how the actions of one person can make a difference and that it's everyone's job to care for the school environment.

2. ROLE PLAYING

Model It

Do a personal inventory. What are some ways that you can take better care of the school environment? Do you waste water, litter, or leave the lights on? If the amount of your garbage increases, do you just get another garbage can or do you recycle more and buy less?

Oversee the School Environment

Parenting Activities

3. TABLE TALK
Talk About It

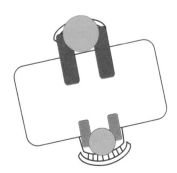

Discuss the following with your child:
- Let's think of some things we can do to use fewer "throw–aways." (1) Write on both sides of the paper. (2) Use cloth instead of paper napkins. (3) Use sponges instead of paper towels. (4) When we go grocery shopping, take canvas bags that we can use over and over instead of paper or plastic bags. (5) Use a lunch box instead of paper bags to pack lunches.

4. WRITING
Recycle?

This book belongs to:

Act as scribe while your child explains why she thinks recycling is important. Then, brainstorm with her what your family can do to recycle. Make a list and share it with everyone. Begin recycling!

August

Parenting Activities

5. PHYSICAL

Taking Inventory

Have your child help you make a list of things your family could do to take better care of the school environment. Use the checklist on page 91 to keep track. Then, one by one, decide what you will do about them.

6. READING

Finding Help

Read *Mrs. Honey's Tree* by Pam Adams with your child. Talk about how Mrs. Honey helped the mayor consider another solution by calling attention to the problem, stopping the action before it was too late, and finding someone who could help. Are there any environmental issues in your child's school that he can help with?

Children's Stories

Oversee the School Environment

Parenting Activities

7. COMMUNITY

Recycle It

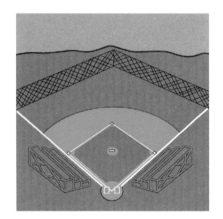

Some people call the United States a "throw away" society because we buy so much that we have to keep throwing it away to make room for more and because there is so much plastic packaging. We just don't think about how much we use and how much we throw away. Talk over the following recycling ideas with your child and decide which ones your family can do. (1) Donate unwanted items to the *Salvation Army*, *Goodwill*, or *Habitat for Humanity*. (2) Shop at "good–as–new" shops. (3) Hand down the clothes and toys your child has outgrown. (4) Have a yard sale to get rid of things you don't use anymore.

Successful Parenting Practices

- Help your child become aware of how much she consumes. For instance, use a dosage cup that comes with cough medicine to measure out the amount of shampoo your child needs. When you're getting fast food, only take the items you need (a straw, a napkin or two, or a spoon). Limit the time for showers.

Copyright© 2006 "I Care" Products & Services   (2nd Grade)

Oversee the School Environment

Activity 1: Physical–Taking Inventory

Have your child help you to make a list of things your family could do to take better care of the environment. Use the checklist below to keep track. Then, one by one, decide what you will do about them.

How Kind Are We to the Environment?

How many electrical appliances and equipment are turned on all of the time? (The only appliances that need to be turned on all the time are security systems and refrigerators.) **What can we do?**

How many appliances are plugged in all the time, even if they are turned off? (Even if an appliance is turned off, it is using energy. Up to 15% of our electric bill is from things in "standby" mode.) **What can we do?**

How much newspaper do you throw away without even reading it? (It takes one 10– year–old tree to make the newspaper used each year by an average family.) **What can we do?**

How many cans, glass, and plastic do you throw away each week? (22% of the cost of food is for packaging and wrapping.) **What can we do?**

How much food do you throw away? (For some families, up to 50% of the trash is uneaten food.) **What can we do?**

Oversee the School Environment

Enrichment Activity

Activity 2: Art–Gift Wrapping

Have you ever thought about how much gift wrapping gets thrown away every year? Ask your child to make a supply of gift wrapping for you from old newspapers, 20 sheets or more. She can use markers, crayons, tempera paint, Koolaid©, or food dye to decorate them. If you use anything to dye the paper, take great care not to tear it during the dying process. You may want to put several sheets together to make it stronger. Make sure the paper is flat while it is drying. She can make some for different occasions such as weddings, anniversaries, a new baby, or just everyday wrapping paper.

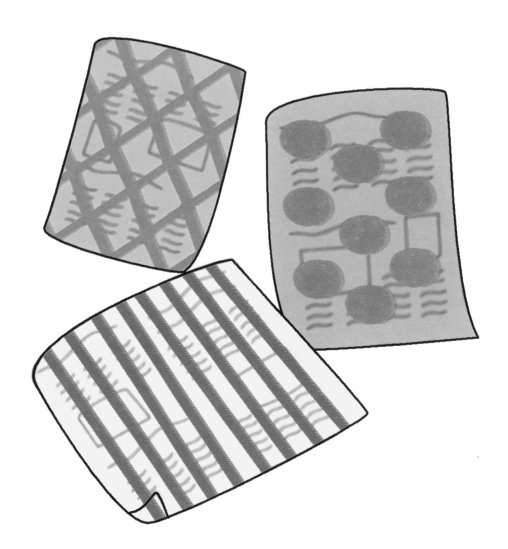

Oversee the School Environment

Activity 3: Project–Back to School Party

Making school important to your child can be rewarding and fun. Give your child a Back–to–School Party. Ask her to design the party invitation to send to her friends. She can cut out and use the invitation below as a guide.

You're Invited!

School is going to be fun this year!

Cut out the invitation below to use as an example for the Project Activity.

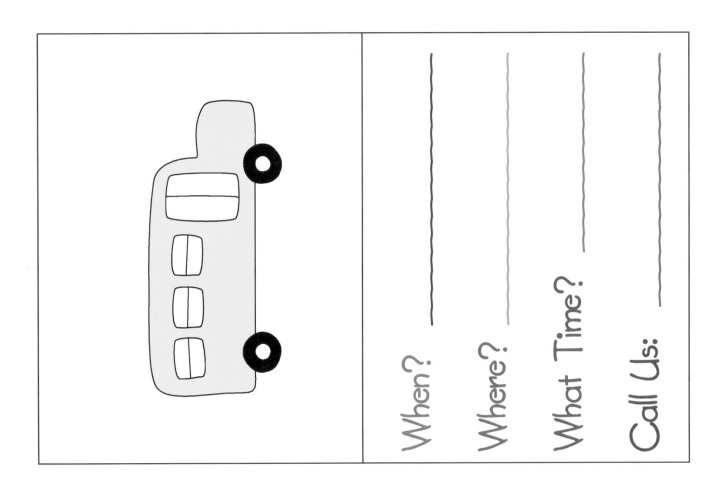

Oversee the School Environment

Activity 4: Visual Learning

Together with your child, list ways in the "Free Space" below that she can make a difference at school. Post the message in a visible location for your child to see it often during the month. At the end of the month, complete *Activity 5* on the other side of this sheet.

One person can make a difference.

Free Space

_____

_____

_____

_____

_____

August

Oversee the School Environment

Reinforcement Activity

Activity 5: Things I Like About School

Record things your child likes about school and post in a visible location.

1. _____

2. _____

3. _____

4. _____

5. _____

Oversee the School Environment

Activity 6: Reflection Log

Summarize your child's positive interactions during the month and reward yourself for a job well done.

Child's Name _____ **Date** _____

Name of Parent(s) _____

Record the number for each of the following questions in the box on the right.

A. How many of the workbook activities did you do with your child?

B. How many positive recognitions did your child receive from teachers, family members, friends, etc.?

C. How many positive recognitions did your child receive from you, the parent(s)?

Oversee the School Environment

D. Record five self–initiated positive activities you did with your child that were not in this month's workbook activities.

1. _____

_____

2. _____

_____

3. _____

_____

4. _____

_____

5. _____

_____

Message to Parents

Teachers and parents alike complain that children don't listen. Sometimes the problem is one of motivation. And at other times, children don't know how to focus on the message in the words. Help your child become a good listener by improving his motivation and his skill.

1. COMMUNICATION

Listen Up

Listening is more than being quiet when someone is talking. It is trying to understand what they are saying. Talk with your child about the importance of listening and what happens when people don't. Use problem solving, such as the following, to illustrate the difference between hearing and listening. *You are driving a bus. You go east 10 miles, turn north for two miles, and pick up seven passengers. Then, you turn west and go two miles and let off four passengers. How old is the bus driver?*

2. ROLE PLAYING

Model It

Practice good listening skills yourself. Look at your child and get down on his level. Ask him to repeat what you have said to see if he understood what you were saying and what you meant. Offer nonverbal and verbal responses to what he says.

Parenting Activities

3. TABLE TALK

Talk About It

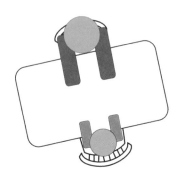

Discuss the following with your child:
- What are some of the things that make it hard for you to listen?
- Do you think there are times when you don't have to listen? What are they? Is that right?
- How can you tell if someone is listening just by looking at them?
- Why is it easier to listen sometimes and not others?
- What does it feel like when someone won't listen to you?
- Tell me what I just said.

4. WRITING

Listening Ears

Cut out the templates on page 105. On each one, have your child write down a tip for good listening. Then, cut out the cover on page 103 (you child can even decorate it) and staple them all together in book fashion. Keep it where he can refer to it. Some of the tips might be: (1) keep looking at the person who's speaking; (2) don't interrupt; (3) sit still; (4) nod your head if you agree with something; (5) lean toward the speaker; (6) repeat instructions and ask appropriate questions when the speaker has finished.

Listening

Parenting Activities

5. PHYSICAL

What Did He Say?

On average, American kids spend 4.5 hours a day in front of a screen, whether it is a TV, DVD, video game, or computer. One result is poor listening skills. Try this activity to get away from the television and reinforce good listening. With everyone sitting around a table, each person, in turn, describes his favorite movie and tells why it is his favorite. Then, when everyone has had a turn, go around the circle again and this time tell what someone else had said in round one. Continue until everyone has had a turn. On round three, have each person recall both someone else's favorite movie and television show. Keep going with different kinds of favorites for as long as you can.

6. READING

Listening to Your Child

Children's Stories

Children love to play with language. Keeping that love alive as they get older will make them better readers and writers. When you first read *Drummer Hoff* by Barbara Emberley with your child, use different tempo, loudness, and tone for each character. Turn the reading over to your child and encourage him to be as expressive as he can be.

Parenting Activities

7. COMMUNITY

What Was That?

Take a car ride with your child. Blindfold him so he can't see where you are going. Go somewhere that has distinctive sounds, like an automatic car wash, a road with lots of traffic, a fast food drive–thru, or by a park where kids are playing. Ask him to describe where you are from what he hears, giving as much detail as possible.

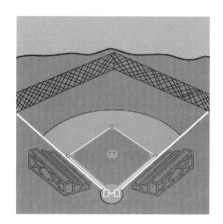

Successful Parenting Practices

- Restating or rephrasing what children have said shows them that you were listening. It also verifies that you heard them correctly. Having them tell you what they have heard helps them develop the skill of reflective listening.

Enrichment Activity

Activity 1: Writing–Listening Ears

Use the cover and templates below for the *Writing Activity* on page 100.

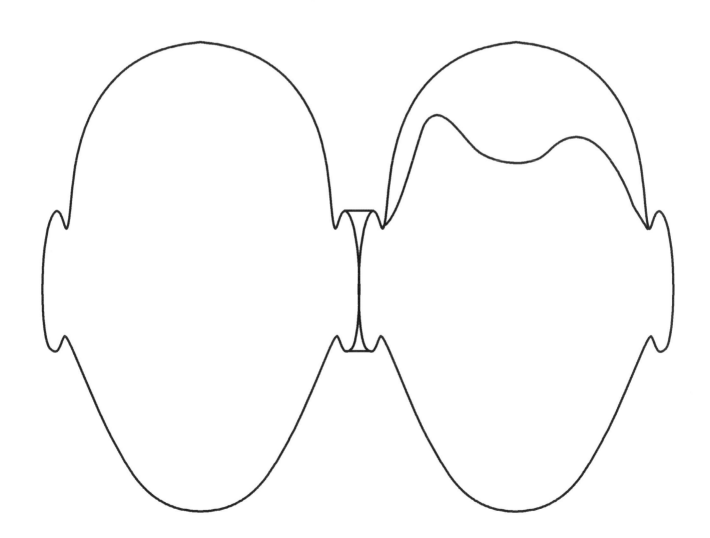

Cut out the book cover on the other side of this page for the Writing Activity

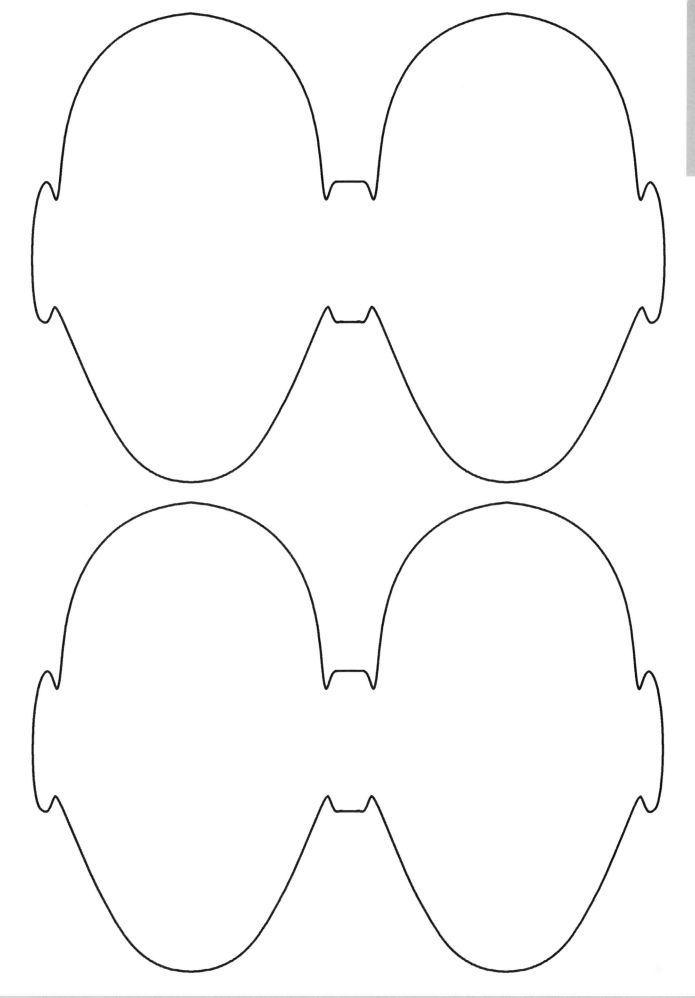

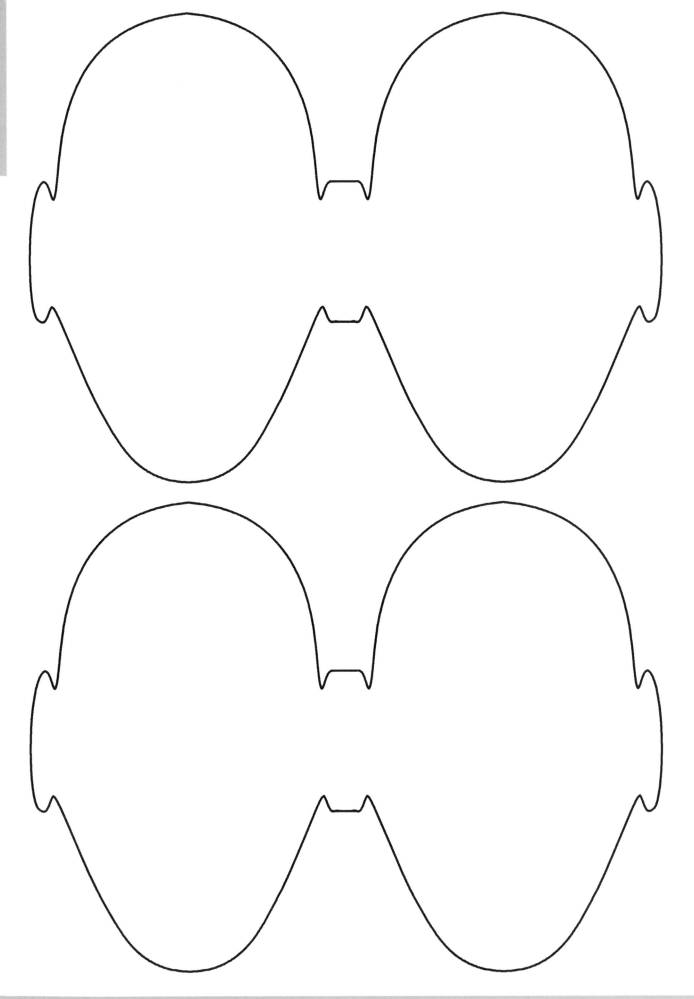

Listening

Activity 2: Project—Listening Challenge

To highlight the importance of listening, challenge your child to listen carefully for an entire day; perhaps a weekend when you will be spending a lot of time together. Tell him that throughout the day, you will mention some numbers and if he hears them, he should write them down on his tally sheet. At the end of the day, he will receive dollars to match the total of the numbers you have said, but only if he has the total correct. Warn him that you will be saying plus or minus before the numbers. All he has to do is write down what he hears. You will help him total the numbers later. (Hint: you may want to practice saying the numbers within a sentence. It is harder than you think.) You'll find examples below, along with the tally sheet on the next page.

Say is like this:

- Josh, please set the *plus two* table so that we can eat lunch.
- I've got to go to the store to *minus three* pick up the nails for the project. Do you want to come along?

Show your child how to record the numbers:

Numbers I Heard

1. +3

2. -1

Consolation prize

If your child doesn't hear all of the numbers, give him a consolation prize for trying. Then, try the activity another day. Keep trying until he gets them all.

Numbers: +4, +1, +4, -2, +1, -3, +2, -1, -1, +2
Total = 7

Listening

Numbers I Heard	Numbers I Heard

Numbers I Heard

1.

2.

3.

4.

5.

6.

7.

8.

9.

10.

Total=

Numbers I Heard

1.

2.

3.

4.

5.

6.

7.

8.

9.

10.

Total=

Positive Message

Activity 3: Visual Learning

Discuss with your child the importance of listening rather than just talking. Post the message in a visible location for your child to see it often during the month. At the end of the month, complete *Activity 4* on the other side of this sheet.

You can learn more from listening than from talking.

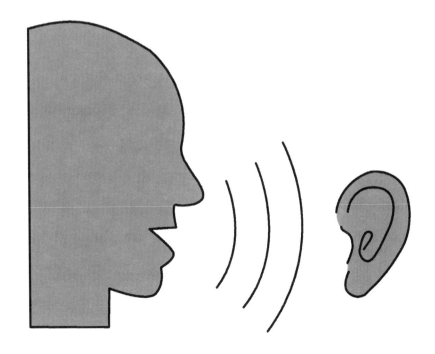

Listening

Reinforcement Activity

Activity 4: Stories I Like to Listen to . . .

Record some of the stories your child likes to listen to and post in a visible location.

1. _____

2. _____

3. _____

4. _____

5. _____

Activity 5: Reflection Log

Summarize your child's positive interactions during the month and reward yourself for a job well done.

Child's Name _____ **Date** _____

Name of Parent(s) _____

Record the number for each of the following questions in the box on the right.

A. How many of the workbook activities did you do with your child?

B. How many positive recognitions did your child receive from teachers, family members, friends, etc.?

C. How many positive recognitions did your child receive from you, the parent(s)?

Listening

D. Record five self–initiated positive activities you did with your child that were not in this month's workbook activities.

1. _____

_____

2. _____

_____

3. _____

_____

4. _____

_____

5. _____

_____

September

Copyright© 2006 "I Care" Products & Services   (2nd Grade)

Parenting Activities

Message to Parents

Optimism can be learned. It's been shown that children develop either optimistic or pessimistic reactions to things based on what they have observed. What you think and what you do equals to how you feel.

1. COMMUNICATION

Pessimism vs Optimism

Research shows that people who are pessimistic have a much greater chance of having a heart attack, developing cancer, or dying younger than optimists. Pessimists don't take care of themselves as well as optimists because they feel it won't do any good. Help your child develop an understanding of the difference between optimism and pessimism. Tell her they are ready to learn some "big words" that really mean thinking things will be okay and thinking things will not be okay. Use the chart on page 117, adding any other ideas you or your child come up with.

2. ROLE PLAYING

Model It

Because optimism is learned from role models, it is important that you are optimistic yourself. Stay calm when things don't go right. Worrying won't solve problems. Besides, children are quick to sense your worry and start to worry themselves.

Optimism

Parenting Activities

3. TABLE TALK

Talk About It

Discuss the following with your child:
- Use encouraging words with your child: "You almost did it!"; "You can do it!"; "Try again."; "Don't give up."; "You did it better this time."; "You're on the right track now!"
- Talk over the following sayings: (1) Dwelling on negative thoughts is like fertilizing weeds. (2) Practice hope. (3) A positive attitude can make dreams come true. (4) Those who wish to sing always find a song.

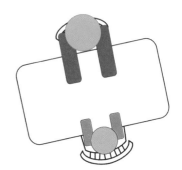

4. WRITING

A Spoonful of Sugar

Can anyone be more optimistic than *Mary Poppins*? Watch the movie with your child, then discuss such questions as the following: (1) How could she be so positive all of the time? (2) What did she do about problems? Help your child come up with some ways to think more positively about something at home or at school.

Copyright© 2006 "I Care" Products & Services (2nd Grade)

Optimism

Parenting Activities

5. PHYSICAL

I Can Do It

Research shows that achievement is more effective than verbal encouragement in developing an optimistic attitude. The sense of accomplishment leads to positive expectations for the future. Help your child identify and carry out a task or project that will lead to a sense of accomplishment. It might be taking dancing lessons or learning new soccer kicks. How about setting up a challenge to read a book every night for two weeks or send a card to every grandparent by the end of the week. Make sure it is achievable.

6. READING

A Good Thing

Children's Stories

Harold was out one night with his purple crayon, happily creating one adventure after another. He didn't worry about being lost or running into monsters. After reading *Harold and the Purple Crayon* by Crockett Johnson with your child, talk about how Harold's positive attitude was a good thing.

October

Optimism

Parenting Activities

7. COMMUNITY

About the Community

Use the worksheet on page 118 to help your child create an advertisement encouraging people to visit your community because it is such a good place to live. Help her find positive things she can boast about. If she needs help, act as scribe.

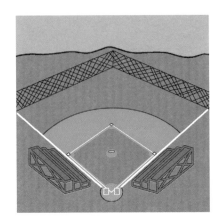

Successful Parenting Practices

- Kids learn to ignore what you say if you are always assuring them things are alright when they are not alright to them. Remember to deal with the facts.

116

Enrichment Activity

Activity 1: Communication–Pessimism vs Optimism

Use the chart below for the *Communication Activity* on page 113.

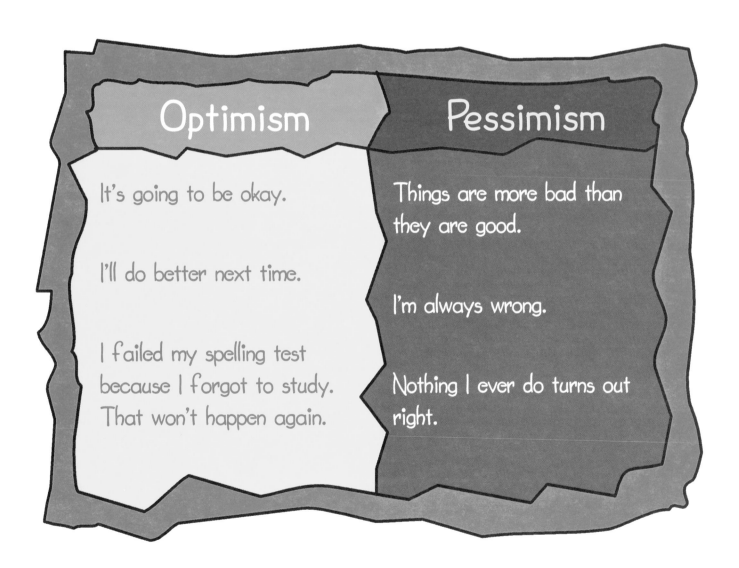

Optimism	Pessimism
It's going to be okay.	Things are more bad than they are good.
I'll do better next time.	I'm always wrong.
I failed my spelling test because I forgot to study. That won't happen again.	Nothing I ever do turns out right.

Optimism

Enrichment Activity

Activity 2: Community–What's Good

Use the worksheet below for the *Community Activity* on page 116. Have your child write the reasons your town is great in the rays of the sun. Your child can also decorate the figure below.

My town is great because . . .

Enrichment Activity

Activity 3: Project–Let's Look at the Facts

One important technique for teaching optimism is to help your child realize the facts of a situation instead of getting carried away by the feeling that she has done something wrong or things will never get better. The next time a situation comes up in which she feels disappointed or depressed, help her to express what happened, how she feels, and then review the facts. Use the chart below as an example. You can tear out the chart and post it in a visible location. Talk over the examples below with your child, then add some situations of your own. Use this technique whenever the need arises.

Let's Look at the Facts		
What Happened	*How I Feel*	*The Facts*
My brother gets to sleep over and go the movies with his friends. I never can.	My parents don't love me as much as him. They'll never let me do those things.	My brother is four years older than I am. Mom says when he was my age he couldn't sleep over or go to the movies either.
I used to help my teacher with stuff in class. Now she only asks my friend, Sarah.	Mrs. Sweet doesn't like me because I missed school when I was sick. I hate school. I hate Mrs. Sweet.	Mrs. Sweet wants me to take some extra time to make up the work I missed when I was sick. I'll be able to help again when I've caught up.

Copyright© 2006 "I Care" Products & Services   (2nd Grade)   Do Not Photocopy.

Optimism

Tear out this page and display the
Optimism Chart for the Project Activity

right*Optimism*

Positive Message

Activity 4: Visual Learning

Let your child hear you using the phrases below the positive message often. Post the message in a visible location for your child to see it often during the month. At the end of the month, complete *Activity 5* on the other side of this sheet.

Keep a positive attitude.
It will make a difference.

Have a great day!

Everything is going to be alright.

I feel good today!

I know you will do your best.

It's a great day!

Optimism

Reinforcement Activity

Activity 5: The Things I Want to Do . . .

Record some things your child wants to do when she grows up and post in a visible location.

1. _____

2. _____

3. _____

4. _____

5. _____

Copyright© 2006 "I Care" Products & Services   (2nd Grade)

Optimism

Activity 6: Reflection Log

Summarize your child's positive interactions during the month and reward yourself for a job well done.

Child's Name _____ **Date** _____

Name of Parent(s) _____

Record the number for each of the following questions in the box on the right.

A. How many of the workbook activities did you do with your child? ☐

B. How many positive recognitions did your child receive from teachers, family members, friends, etc.? ☐

C. How many positive recognitions did your child receive from you, the parent(s)? ☐

Copyright© 2006 "I Care" Products & Services   (2nd Grade)

Optimism

D. Record five self–initiated positive activities you did with your child that were not in this month's workbook activities.

1. _____

   _____

2. _____

   _____

3. _____

   _____

4. _____

   _____

5. _____

   _____

Parenting Activities

Message to Parents

Children need to learn to act fairly in order to get along with others. You can begin by helping your child to understand what fairness is.

1. COMMUNICATION

What Is Fairness?

What is fairness? It's not always getting your "fair share." It is not everyone having the same rights. It is everyone having what is right for them and for others. That's why it's not always easy to determine what is fair. One way to make "fairness" easier to understand is to establish some rules. Go over the "Rules of Fairness" with your child that are listed on page 129. Praise him when he follows the rules and remind him when he doesn't

2. ROLE PLAYING

Model It

In our culture, there is an emphasis on equal rights. This can make it difficult to be fair. Let your child see that you are trying to be fair. Explain your decisions and point out what is right for each person.

Fairness

Parenting Activities

3. TABLE TALK

Talk About It

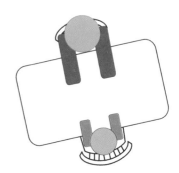

Discuss the following with your child:
- How do you know when something is unfair?
- How should you treat people who are not fair with you?
- What would be a fair way for two children to share a bike?
- When you're a good sport, what do other kids think of you?
- Give me some examples of not being fair with others.

4. WRITING

What I've Learned

Help your child make a record of the things he learned about fairness. You can use page 130. Tear out the page and hang it to remind him of how important fairness is.

Fairness

Parenting Activities

5. PHYSICAL

Fair Play

Fairness means treating others the way you want to be treated. Fair–minded people play by the rules and don't take advantage of others. Play a game with your child. Go over the rules carefully and then break a few while you are playing. How does your child react? Use this as an opportunity to talk about fair play and treating others the way we want to be treated.

6. READING

Politeness Plan

Children's Stories

Read *The Berenstain Bears Forget Their Manners* by Stan and Jan Berenstain with your child. Then, talk with your child about whether your family needs a "Politeness Plan." If so, make one and share it with the entire family. Then stick to it, penalties and all.

Fairness

Parenting Activities

7. COMMUNITY

The Right Thing to Do

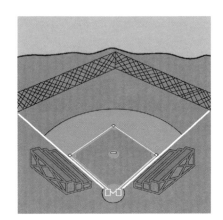

Being fair does not mean treating everyone equally. It means doing what's right. For instance, some people think it's not fair that disabled people have special parking spaces and they don't. But it's the right thing to do. Some people believe it's not fair to have shelters for the homeless or give food and money to some people and not to others. Use these examples to help your child understand that fairness does not always mean treating everyone the same.

Successful Parenting Practices

- Parents must realize that, in order to be fair to their children, each must be treated differently. We must recognize their unique patterns of strengths and needs.

Fairness

Activity 1: Communication-Rules of Fairness

Use the rules below for the *Communication Activity* on page 125.

Rules of Fairness

✳ Don't play favorites. ✳

✳ Know and follow the rules. ✳

✳ Don't take more than
your fair share. ✳

✳ Don't put the blame on
others when it's your fault. ✳

✳ Treat other people the way
you want to be treated. ✳

✳ Don't take advantage of people. ✳

Copyright© 2006 "I Care" Products & Services   (2nd Grade)

129
Do Not Photocopy.

Fairness

Enrichment Activity

Activity 2: Writing–What I've Learned

Use the space below for the *Writing Activity* on page 126.

What I've Learned About Fairness

_____

_____

_____

_____

_____

_____

_____

_____

_____

Enrichment Activity

Activity 3: Project—What Do You Think?

Some people might think that 2nd graders are too young to discuss matters of fairness in depth. Experience says otherwise. The more their thinking is challenged, the more they think, and the more they think in depth. The next time your child has friends over, sit them down at the table, give them a snack to munch on, and tell them you want them to do some thinking with you. Use the questions below about "Getting Even." Then, record and review their responses. Tell them what a good job of thinking they did.

Getting Even—What Do You Think?

Directions: Go over the following questions with your child and his friends. Ask for their opinions. Push their thinking by saying "Why do you think that?" or "Tell me more." If they can't, that's okay. Remember, there are no right or wrong answers.

When someone treats you badly, do you ever try to "get even" by doing something bad to him? Why?

Does that really make things even? Why do you think that?

What might happen if we try to get even? Will this make the other person want to "get even" back? Then what?

What does "Two wrongs don't make a right" mean?

Is there a difference between trying to "get even" and trying to "teach someone a lesson"?

Fairness

November

Enrichment Activity

Activity 4: Project—Taking Turns

Discuss the importance of taking turns with your child when he is involved in a group activity or playing with friends. One fun way to teach this skill is by playing the game "Tic, Tac, Toe" with your child often. You can use the templates below to get started.

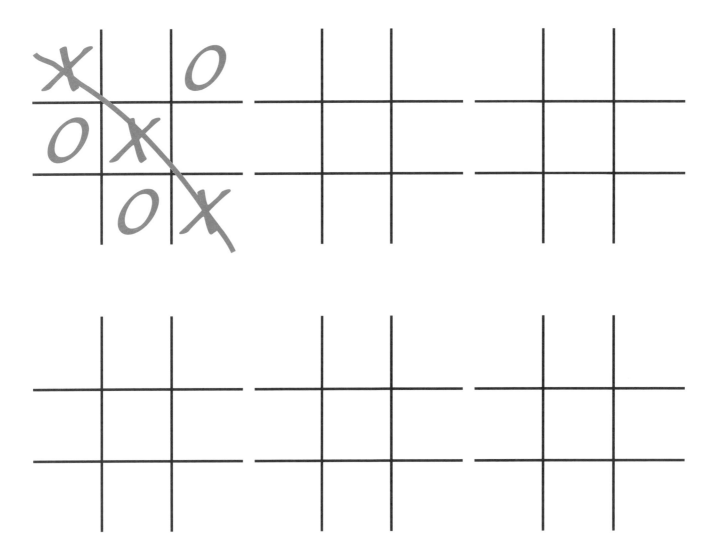

Copyright© 2006 "I Care" Products & Services   (2nd Grade)

Activity 5: Visual Learning

Discuss and circle the fairness phrases below the positive message. Post the message in a visible location for your child to see it often during the month. At the end of the month, complete *Activity 6* on the other side of this sheet.

Be fair to others and they will be fair to you.

Excuse me.

May I?

Get it yourself!

It's your turn.

Can I?

You're welcome.

Do you mind?

Thank you.

It's mine!

Reinforcement Activity

Activity 6: How I Treat Others . . .

Record times your child has demonstrated fairness and post in a visible location.

1. _____

2. _____

3. _____

4. _____

5. _____

Copyright© 2006 "I Care" Products & Services   (2nd Grade)

Fairness

Activity 7: Reflection Log

Summarize your child's positive interactions during the month and reward yourself for a job well done.

Child's Name _____ **Date** _____

Name of Parent(s) _____

Record the number for each of the following questions in the box on the right.

A. How many of the workbook activities did you do with your child? ☐

B. How many positive recognitions did your child receive from teachers, family members, friends, etc.? ☐

C. How many positive recognitions did your child receive from you, the parent(s)? ☐

Copyright© 2006 "I Care" Products & Services   (2nd Grade)   Do Not Photocopy.

Fairness

D. Record five self–initiated positive activities you did with your child that were not in this month's workbook activities.

1. _____

_____

2. _____

_____

3. _____

_____

4. _____

_____

5. _____

_____

Parenting Activities

Message to Parents

Loyalty is about honoring your commitments to family and friends. Help your child realize that, although being loyal is not always easy, it's worth it. You have the satisfaction of knowing you did the right thing and you earn the trust and loyalty of others.

1. COMMUNICATION

Examples of Loyalty

Help your child develop an understanding of loyalty by discussing examples of loyalty and comparing them to examples of disloyalty. See list on page 141.

2. ROLE PLAYING

Model It

Show your loyalty to family and friends. Keep your commitments. Spend time with them and voice your support for what they do. Listen when they need someone to talk to. Don't let your busy schedule get in the way.

Loyalty

Parenting Activities

3. TABLE TALK

Talk About It

Discuss the following with your child:

- Sometimes your friends ask you to do something you know isn't right. If you say no to your friend, it's okay. You're not being disloyal. People have no right to ask someone else to do something wrong.
- What are some of the ways animals can be loyal to people? What can we learn from that?
- Talk to your child about situations in which people should be loyal (i.e. when someone tries to get you to stop being friends with someone else). Also discuss when being loyal is not a good idea (i.e. when someone is abusing you or breaking the rules).

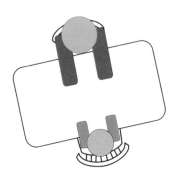

4. WRITING

Ways to Be Loyal

Ask your child to think of some of the ways she can be loyal to the family and to her friends. Write them down and post them. During the month, talk about what she's doing to show her loyalty.

Copyright© 2006 "I Care" Products & Services   (2nd Grade)

Parenting Activities

5. PHYSICAL

Decisions, Decisions

Help your child act out the following scenarios, coming up with a solutions. (1) You have a new friend that you really enjoy doing things with. This friend doesn't like your oldest friend and tells you not to play with or hang around that person. (2) You've made a promise to attend a party, but your cousin just called and asked you to go to the new movie you want to see.

6. READING

Love and Loyalty

Children's Stories

The Emperor and the Kite by Jane Yolan is a story about love and loyalty. After reading it with your child, talk about ways that the members of your family show loyalty toward each other, and ways they can show loyalty in the future.

Parenting Activities

7. COMMUNITY

Community Hero

Help your child identify and research someone in the community who is a loyal citizen, who cares for the people in the community, and who tries to help them. Call the office of your local newspaper or go to the library to find out about this person. You can help your child complete the form on page 142 to summarize what she found out.

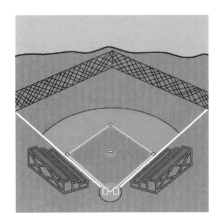

Successful Parenting Practices

- Help your child understand that you can be loyal to someone and still disagree with some of the things he or she does.

Loyalty

Enrichment Activity

Activity 1: Communication–Examples of Loyalty

Use the list below for the *Communication Activity* on page 137.

Examples of Loyalty	*Examples of Disloyalty*
• Keeping your promise to go to a friend's house even though you have a chance to go to a cool movie.	• Not sticking up for your oldest friend when someone makes fun of her.
• Being a good friend.	• Telling a secret that someone has asked you not to.
• Standing up for those you care about.	• Doing anything just so others will like you.
• Keeping secrets of those who trust you.	• Asking a friend to do something wrong or spreading gossip that could hurt others.

December

Loyalty

Enrichment Activity

Activity 2: Community–Community Hero

Use the form below for the *Community Activity* on page 140.

Who is your community hero?

_____

_____

When and where was this person born?

_____

_____

What has this person done to help your community?

_____

_____

Why do you think this person is a hero?

_____

_____

Loyalty

Activity 3: Project—Loyal to My Heritage

Many people have great loyalty to their cultural heritage. Help your child learn more about her heritage. Go online or to the library to find out about the country or cultural group you come from. Have your child record some of the interesting facts she learned below and draw a picture of something significant from the culture.

_____

_____

_____

_____

Copyright© 2006 "I Care" Products & Services   (2nd Grade)

Loyalty

Enrichment Activity

Activity 4: Project–Symbols of Loyalty

Most countries use flags as a symbol to promote loyalty. Below are some flags and the countries they represent.

Canada

South Africa

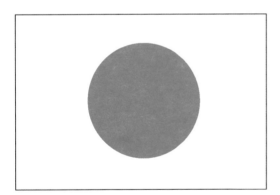

Japan

Switzerland

United States of America

Italy

144
Do Not Photocopy.

Copyright© 2006 "I Care" Products & Services   (2nd Grade)

Loyalty

Activity 5: Visual Learning

In the "Free Space" below the positive message, ask your child to list things she feels passionate about. Post the message in a visible location for your child to see it often during the month. At the end of the month, complete *Activity 6* on the other side of this sheet.

Loyalty is sticking up for someone or something that is important to you.

Free Space

_____

_____

_____

_____

_____

Loyalty

Reinforcement Activity

Activity 6: I Show Loyalty When . . .

Record instances when your child showed loyalty and post in a visible location.

1. _____

2. _____

3. _____

4. _____

5. _____

Copyright© 2006 "I Care" Products & Services   (2nd Grade)

Loyalty

Reflection Activity

Activity 7: Reflection Log

Summarize your child's positive interactions during the month and reward yourself for a job well done.

Child's Name _____ **Date** _____

Name of Parent(s) _____

Record the number for each of the following questions in the box on the right.

A. How many of the workbook activities did you do with your child?

B. How many positive recognitions did your child receive from teachers, family members, friends, etc.?

C. How many positive recognitions did your child receive from you, the parent(s)?

Loyalty

D. Record five self–initiated positive activities you did with your child that were not in this month's workbook activities.

1. _____

   _____

2. _____

   _____

3. _____

   _____

4. _____

   _____

5. _____

   _____

Recommended Books

To order a set of books that corresponds to the Positive Parenting Activities in this Workbook, or to order additional Workbooks from the "Unleash the Greatness in Your Child" Series or "I Care" books (see following pages), fill out the order form below. Then, cut the form along the dotted line and tear out the card along the perforation. Send the card along with check, money order, or credit card information in an envelope and mail it to the address shown on the card. You can also place your order at www.icarenow.com/parents.html, or e–mail the information requested on the card to parents5@icarenow.com.

2nd Grade Book Pack $64.95

Amelia Bedelia
Berenstain Bears Forget Their Manners, The
Charlotte's Web
Drummer Hoff
Emperor and the Kite, The
Harold and the Purple Crayon
I Want to Be a Teacher
Jack's Garden
Magic Fan, The
Mrs. Honey's Tree
Shy Charles
Wings

	$64.95
Tax @ 7%	$4.55
S & H @ 10%	$6.50
Total:	**$76.00**

- -

	Quantity	Price	Total
2nd Grade Book Pack		**$64.95**	
"Unleash the Greatness In Your Child" Workbook Series		**$19.95**	
Indicate Grade Level			
"I Care" Parental Involvement—Engaging Parents to Improve Student Performance Book		**$14.95**	
☐ English _____		Subtotal	
☐ Spanish _____		Tax @ 7%	
		S & H @ $5.00 or 10% (whichever is greater)	
		Grand Total	

Method of Payment:

☐ Check

☐ Money Order

☐ Credit Card

_____
Name on Card

_____
Credit Card Number

_____
Expiration Date

149

Workbook Series

"Unleash the Greatness in Your Child" Workbook Series   **$19.95/ea.**

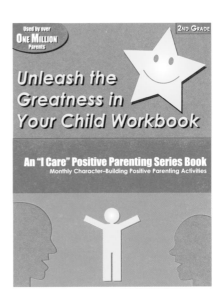

Workbook Grade Level	Available
Toddler	**May 2006**
Pre–Kindergarten	**Now**
Kindergarten	**Now**
1st Grade	**Now**
2nd Grade	**Now**
3rd Grade	**May 2006**
4th Grade	**May 2006**
5th Grade	**May 2006**
6th Grade	**June 2006**
7th Grade	**August 2006**
8th Grade	**August 2006**
9th Grade	**August 2006**
10th Grade	**September 2006**
11th Grade	**September 2006**
12th Grade	**September 2006**

	$19.95
Tax @ 7%	$1.40
S & H @ $5.00 or 10% (whichever is greater)	$5.00
Total:	**$26.35**

- -

Mail to:

_____
Name

_____
Street Address

_____
City   State   ZIP

_____
Telephone (Optional)

_____
E-mail Address (Optional)

"I Care" Parenting Manual
P.O. Box 492
906 Elmo Street
Americus, GA 31709

50 Ways Parents Can Say "I Care"

1. Post & Discuss Positive Messages
2. Attend Teacher/Parent Conferences
3. Take Family Portraits
4. Post Affirmation Pledges
5. Eat Meals Together
6. Post Daily Schedule
7. Assign Chores
8. Make Scrapbooks Together
9. Cook Meals Together
10. Award Certificates
11. Watch Movies Together
12. Visit Theme Parks
13. Volunteer at School
14. Read Books to Each Other
15. Attend Family Events
16. Give Parties for Special Occasions
17. Schedule Board Game Nights
18. Visit the Zoo
19. Help with a Class Project
20. Monitor TV Programs
21. Attend Parenting Workshops
22. Send Get Well Cards to Friends & Family
23. Lunch with Mom
24. Lunch with Dad
25. Encourage Hobbies
26. Attend Sport Events
27. Attend Local Theatre
28. Provide Enrichment Activities
29. Schedule Ice Cream Socials
30. Visit the Library
31. Go Shopping Together
32. Attend Friends' Events
33. Help with Homework
34. Post a Child Affirmation Pledge
35. Enroll Child in Book Club
36. Go Fishing Together
37. Go Skating Together
38. Encourage Creativity
39. Discuss Child's Day
40. Praise Good Efforts
41. Say *I Love You* Often
42. Write Notes to Recognize Achievement
43. Document Positive Activities
44. Talk About Positive Activities
45. Role Model Desired Behaviors
46. Support Extracurricular Activities
47. Schedule Family Nights
48. Attend Community Events
49. Help with School Projects
50. Set Limits

"I Care" Parental Involvement Book

"I Care" Parental Involvement—Engaging Parents to Improve Student Performance, by Elbert D. Solomon, is full of research–based, field–tested implementation practices and measurement tools and introduces an innovative curricular approach to parental involvement that will delight parents, teachers, and students. More importantly, it will improve student performance, help parents to initiate more positive activities with their children at home, and enable educators to get beyond the difficulties of involving parents. Available in English and Spanish.

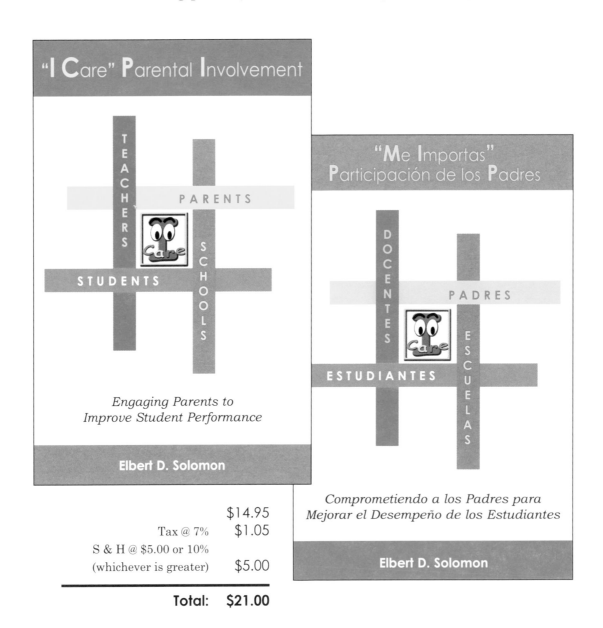

	$14.95
Tax @ 7%	$1.05
S & H @ $5.00 or 10% (whichever is greater)	$5.00
Total:	**$21.00**